Living

in the

Middle

LIVING IN THE MIDDLE

A Life Between Belonging and Becoming

Dr. Samuel S. Dinga

SPEARS BOOKS

Denver, Colorado

Spears Books
An Imprint of Spears Media Press LLC
21699 E. Quincy Ave, Unit F #167
Aurora, CO 80015
United States of America

First Published in the United States of America in 2026 by Spears Books
www.spearsbooks.org
info@spearsmedia.com
Information on this title: https://spearsbooks.org/product/
living-in-the-middle/

© 2026 Samuel S. Dinga
All rights reserved.

No part of this publication may be reproduced, distributed, or transmitted
in any form or by any means, including photocopying, recording, or other
electronic or mechanical methods, without the prior written permission of the
publisher, except in the case of brief quotations embodied in critical reviews
and certain other noncommercial uses permitted by copyright law.
For permission requests, write to the publisher, addressed "Attention:
Permissions Coordinator," at the above address.

Publisher's Cataloging-in-Publication Data

Names: Dinga, Samuel S.
Title: Living in the Middle / Samuel S. Dinga.
Identifiers: ISBN 978-1-957296-81-4 (paperback) | ISBN 978-1-957296-82-1
(ebook)
Subjects: LCSH: Dinga, Samuel S. | Cameroonians—United States—Biography.
| Immigrants—United States—Biography. | Identity (Psychology)—United
States. | Assimilation (Sociology)—United States. | Racially mixed families—
Wisconsin. | Racism—United States. | Bali Nyonga (Cameroon)—Biography.
| Wisconsin—Biography. | BISAC: BIOGRAPHY & AUTOBIOGRAPHY /
Personal Memoirs. | SOCIAL SCIENCE / Emigration & Immigration.
Classification: LCC E184.A24 D56 2026 | DDC 305.896/073092 [B]—dc23
Also available digitally on Kindle, Apple Books, and Google Books

Designed and typeset by Spears Media Press LLC
Cover design: D. Kambem

Dedicated to my dear sister, Makah Rosemary Dinga, who passed away in 2009. You were a kind and gentle soul who taught me the values of kindness, love, and service to others. Your thoughtful way of analyzing every situation inspired me to think deeply about belonging and gave me the strength to complete this project and bring it to life. Continue to rest in peace.

Contents

∗ ∗ ∗

Preface

"There is no greater agony than bearing an untold story inside you."
—*Maya Angelou*

In the hushed dawn of August 17, 1974, the world welcomed not one but two new lives into its embrace. "It's a girl," declared the doctor, but as the room buzzed with anticipation, a second heartbeat echoed, heralding the arrival of a handsome baby boy.

Born in the pre-ultrasound era in Bamenda, Cameroon, my twin sister and I were graced with a heritage rich in tradition and reverence. At a time when twins in some parts of Africa were feared or abandoned, we were cherished, bestowed with names steeped in history and honor: Nah for my sister and Sama for me.

Our birth symbolized more than just two new souls entering the world; it marked a connection to a lineage stretching back to a 14th-century Tikar Kingdom. From fearless leaders to ancient migrations, our family's story is intertwined with the tapestry of Cameroon's history.

Growing up in the village of Bali Nyonga, amid architectural wonders and the echoes of ancestral warriors, I navigated childhood life alongside a bustling family of 20 siblings. Yet despite the love and abundance that surrounded us, my journey would soon take me far from the familiar embrace of home.

Venturing to the United States, I carved a new path, embracing success and happiness, yet grappling with an unshakable sense of displacement. Struggling to reconcile my African roots with my American reality, I found myself caught between worlds, yearning for a place to call home.

Through the pages of this book, I invite you to join me on a quest to unravel the enigma of belonging. From the dusty streets of Cameroon to the quiet corners of Wisconsin, we will explore the complexities of identity, family, and the elusive concept of "home." As we journey together, may we unearth not just answers but a deeper understanding of what it truly means to belong.

CHAPTER 1

Nobility and Lineage

"If you know his father and grandfather, don't worry about his son."
—African proverb

To better understand this chapter, it is important to distinguish between royalty and nobility. Royalty generally refers to the ruling family or dynasty members, including kings (whom we call "Fons"), queens, princes, and princesses. These individuals are typically directly connected to the throne and hold the highest status in the social hierarchy. They embody the identity and continuity of the people, serving as living symbols of tradition and stability. Royal titles are distinct and reserved for those of royal blood, and royal regalia and symbols such as crowns, thrones, and special attire are unique to royalty.

Nobility, on the other hand, refers to individuals who hold high social status and power within society but are not part of the royal family. These individuals often serve as advisors, regional leaders, or officials who support the governance structure. Nobles hold significant social prestige and influence, often derived from their roles, land ownership, or wealth. They may hold administrative positions, such as chiefs, governors, or judges, managing regions or specific functions within the kingdom. While some noble titles and positions can be hereditary, passed down through families, others may be appointed based on merit, loyalty, or service to the royal family.

Understanding these distinctions helps us appreciate the complex social hierarchies and governance structures that have shaped African societies for centuries and will paint a clear picture of my family dynamics. While specifics vary across cultures and regions, the general principles of royalty and nobility provide a framework for understanding their respective roles and significance.

I come from a long line of great men, from my great-grandfather to my grandfather to my father. In his book *In Search of Harmony: A History of Bali Nyonga*, Dr. Ndifontah Nyamndi traces the migration of the Bali Nyonga people, their transformation from a raiding band into a settled community in the Bamenda Grassfields, and their development from a dispirited splinter of the broken Chamba alliance into a structured kingdom with solid institutions and a powerful monarch. He explores the formation and development of the Bali Nyonga kingdom, including the establishment of leadership and governance structures. His book examines the social and political organization of Bali Nyonga, detailing its social hierarchy, the roles of royalty and nobility, and the political institutions that govern the community.

Dr. Nyamndi mentions my great-grandfather, Doh Fongod, who was a sub-chief in his own right. He was a sub-chief of the *Ngod* people who joined the Bali Nyonga clan in Fumban during their migration to their present-day location. One of his daughters married the chief or Fon of Bali Nyonga, Fon Galega I. When she moved to the royal palace to assume her royal duties as queen, she brought along her half-brother Ganwana Fongod, who quickly befriended a young prince, Tita Gwenjang. Both young men were fierce warriors, and Fon Galega I made his son the commander of his army, known as "Mandate," and Ganwana his assistant. Both warriors remained great friends until Prince Tita Gwenjang assumed his father's throne in 1901, becoming Fon Fonyonga II. The new Fon left his compound to his friend Fokum Ganwana and appointed him his *"Nchinted Ngu"* (Head Palace Retainer), to act as the link between the palace and neighboring chiefdoms. It was as a result of this prominence that the title of *Tita Kunted* (Lord of the Palace) in charge of military supplies such as gunpowder and food was conferred upon Ganwana Fongod. Hence, my grandfather Ganwana Fongod became Ba Tita Fokum Ganwana.

Ba Tita Fokum Ganwana was one of the few individuals who held the noble title of *Tita* by affinity (awarded by the palace), rather than by consanguinity (born into the royal bloodline). As a *Tita Kunted* (Lord of the Palace), he was responsible for ensuring that warriors at the battlefront had the necessary supplies, including gunpowder, food, and other provisions. In modern terms, he could be considered a war minister. It is rumored that he married around 84 wives, though some historians claim the number may have reached 100. There are no precise records of how many children he had, but legend suggests that at least 80 of his wives bore children. Ba Tita Fokum Ganwana was a fearless war minister and a close friend of the Fon. After his victorious campaigns in battles, it is said that he would return home with men and princesses from fallen villages. He would then offer some of the princesses in marriage to the Fon and other nobles while keeping some women as his own wives.

In the past, neighboring villages would sometimes send princesses to him as wives, forming alliances to prevent conflicts. Captured fighters and their families were granted land in Bali Nyonga, reminiscent of the Manorial System in medieval Europe or Feudal Systems, where land was given to laborers in exchange for their work. Under these arrangements, families or groups cultivated the land, keeping a portion of the produce for themselves while giving part to Ba Tita Fokum Ganwana, who served as the landlord. While some of these groups still reside in Bali Nyonga, they are no longer required to provide their yields to the descendants of Ba Tita Fokum Ganwana, at least not officially.

When Ba Tita Fokum Ganwana passed away in 1938, his eldest son, Mr. Christian Sama Fokum, inherited the title and became Ba Tita Fokum Christian Sama. The new family head was exiled in 1940 due to his involvement in a chieftaincy dispute following the death of Fon Fonyonga II. After Ba Tita Fokum Christian Sama's exile from Bali Nyonga to Buea and later to Nigeria, his brother, Ba Daiga Fokum (alias Tamali), temporarily led the family. Unfortunately, when Ba Tita Fokum Christian Sama returned from exile, he died at the hospital in Bamenda "Up-Station" before he could reunite with the family. His regent, Ba Daiga Fokum, continued to lead the family until he died in 1970 in Bali Nyonga. His passing left the Fokum clan without a family head.

CHAPTER 2

My Father

A great leader is an ordinary man with extraordinary
wisdom."
—African Proverb

My father, Vincent Dinga Fokum, is one of over a hundred children from the numerous wives of his father, Ba Tita Fokum Ganwana. Despite my grandfather's status as a wealthy noble in his era, the exile of his heir, Ba Christian Sama, led to the confiscation of much of the family land and property, prompting the family to leave Bali Nyonga. As a result, my father was raised in profound poverty, compounded by his father's early death and the family's dispersion across the country following the exile of its patriarch. Fearing potential confrontations and reprisals, some family members even changed their last names.

Vincent Dinga Fokum, my father, was born in 1932 in the Ntaiton quarter of Bali Nyonga, to Ba Tita Fokum Ganwana and Na Nyumia Martha Fokum. He began his education at the Bali vernacular school in Ntanfoang, affiliated with the Basel Mission Church, where he learned to read and write Mungaka, the local language spoken in Bali Nyonga, for about two years. He then continued his schooling at the Basel Mission Elementary School in both Bali and Bafut around 1939. Later, he transferred to St. Joseph's School in Mankon, Bamenda. However, his education was interrupted for two years when he accompanied his father's successor, Ba Tita Fokum Christian Sama, to Buea in the South-West Region of Cameroon in 1940 during the family exodus.

Ba Tita Fokum Christian Sama became embroiled in a dispute over chieftaincy and succession in the Bali Nyonga Fondom, which led to his exile; during that exile, my father and some family members accompanied him. Life in exile was harsh, and after two years, my father decided to return home. He embarked on an arduous 367 km journey on foot, walking from Buea back to Bali Nyonga.

My father returned to school and completed the Standard Six Course in 1948. Upon graduation, he was employed as a pupil teacher at the Bagangu (Akum) Catholic Mission School. He was later transferred to St. Joseph's Parish in Mankon in the same capacity and was promoted to Part "C" until he resigned in December 1951.

In January 1952, he enlisted in the Nigerian Police Force. At the time, the Southern Cameroons was a United Nations trust territory administered by the British as an integral part of Nigeria. Vincent was sent to Ikeja, Lagos, for six months of basic training. He then pursued a career in the police force, rising through every rank until his retirement as Principal Police Commissioner or Senior Superintendent of Police. His final role in the force was as a professor at the Police Academy, where he taught Criminology, Police Investigation, and

Professional Ethics. He retired honorably in 1989 after receiving about twelve commendations for his zeal, integrity, and detective skills. For his meritorious services, he was awarded the Cameroonian Order of Merit, 3rd Class Medal, in 1972, and the Knight of the Order of Valor in 1983.

He stands about 6'2" tall, with a commanding presence, dark complexion, and strikingly handsome features. Clad in his police commissioner uniform, adorned with five bright stars on his shoulders, he exudes an aura of authority that often makes people feel uneasy in his presence. However, beneath this imposing exterior lies a gentle, intelligent, and deeply caring man. He has a fondness for visiting family members, no matter where they are, and always arrives bearing gifts, however modest. He possesses a remarkable breadth of knowledge and seems well-versed in nearly every topic that arises in conversation.

He has immense reverence for medical doctors, often taking us to the hospital for even the slightest health concerns. Throughout his life, he harbored a fervent desire for one of his 20 children to pursue a career in medicine. Though this aspiration went unfulfilled among his offspring, he beamed with pride when his granddaughter, Dr. Bernice Mbongoh, achieved her dream of becoming a medical doctor in 2020.

Similarly, he aspired for one of us to become a lawyer, a goal I shared as I embarked on my university journey in 1997. He frequently emphasized the importance of legal expertise, believing that while wealth and land could be acquired, one could still be outmaneuvered without proper legal counsel. This ambition was realized through my older sister, Cathrine Dinga, whose dedication led her to become a barrister solicitor in 2020.

Most people who crossed paths with him often describe him as a stern, quick-witted, and almost flawless police officer. As a child, I understood the gravity of his role. He held a position of great importance in a perilous profession, as evidenced by the firearm he carried each day he went to work. His duty station was in the coastal city of Victoria (now Limbe), situated along the shores of the Atlantic Ocean. At that point in his career, he served as the police commissioner of the judicial police.

Typically, my father returned home promptly for lunch and a brief respite. However, one day, he failed to arrive, nor did he offer any communication. As the afternoon waned, an alarming news bulletin aired over the radio: armed robbers had launched an assault on the local brewery, resulting in a fierce exchange of gunfire involving law enforcement. The media relayed updates to the community, but uncertainty gripped our household as we anxiously awaited word on my father's well-being.

At some point, my mother and stepmother (my dad's third wife) sent us outside to play, away from the radio. They made several phone calls to the police station, but there was no definitive answer to help calm the fear and worry that consumed our house that afternoon. It was hard to eat dinner, and we even got a free pass on our homework.

As we gathered in the living room around 11:00 p.m., the doorbell's chime pierced the air, freezing us all in place for an instant. I can't recall who answered the door, but I distinctly remember the flood of relief that washed over me when I saw my father standing there, his clothes stained with blood. It was a moment of sheer joy. We rushed toward him, enveloping him in tight embraces—my mother, my stepmother, my siblings, and even the household helpers who had stayed behind to care for us. After the initial reunion, my father instructed us to prepare for bed before retiring to his room. Later, I could overhear snippets of conversation as he recounted the day's harrowing events to the adults who had gathered to listen.

The following morning, we followed our usual routine: getting ready, having breakfast, and being driven to school. Upon our arrival, it seemed like everyone wanted to hug us or greet us with broad smiles. While I was not sure about my twin sister and half-brother, Peter's experiences, my class teacher entered with a beaming smile, hailing my father as a hero for his bravery against the villains the day before. Though I wasn't fully informed about the details, I began to relish my newfound celebrity.

During recess, the older students, usually aloof, invited me to join them for a game of soccer, which was an unprecedented gesture. When the day ended, I excitedly recounted my experiences to my siblings, who shared similar stories of kind treatment. Back home, we shared our day's events with our mothers, who filled in the missing pieces of the story. We were filled with pride to learn that our father and his colleagues had thwarted a robbery at the local brewery, resulting in the capture and demise of two criminals. His heroism garnered media attention for weeks, and on National Day, he was awarded a medal, with another star later added to his uniform.

He helped many people throughout his career. He often spoke about reviewing the files of those detained under his care to ensure they were not wrongfully held for frivolous reasons. He sometimes asked my mother to prepare food for the detainees and made sure they were treated humanely. It is no wonder that he stood out as a leader in the family when the time came.

In March 1970, following the passing of the family regent and the absence of a family head, the family convened in Bamenda at the residence of their elder sibling, Mr. Joseph Lumvalla Fokum, to determine the next family leader. They established specific criteria for the ideal candidate, prioritizing youth and education. After careful deliberation, a vote was held among three candidates who met these criteria. My father emerged as the chosen leader by majority vote. Subsequently, he assumed the title of Ba Tita Fokum. This method of selection was notably unique in Bali Nyonga, representing a departure from the traditional hereditary or incumbent-leader selection process in favor of a democratic election.

As the head of the Fokum family, my father, along with the rest of the family, agreed to return home to Bali Nyonga after most of the family had been scattered across the country during the exile of his predecessor, Ba Tita Fokum Christian Sama. The family decided to rebuild the family compound as a symbol of their return and readiness to take their place in the village.

During their prolonged absence, certain members of the royal family had occupied the family compound. In response, my father, a young, dynamic, and educated police officer, diligently drafted legal briefs presented in court against those who had encroached on the family lands throughout the village, including the family compound. Eventually, he was granted ownership of the family land, along with all the rights and privileges associated with his title as the Lord of the

Palace. To this day, our family still benefits from this nobility under the auspices of my father's fearless servant-leadership.

Over the years, his responsibilities have included ensuring that his brothers' children, scattered across the world during the exile, can own a piece of the recovered family land. He also presides over family marriages, names children and grandchildren, oversees burial rites and celebrations, and conducts annual family meetings, all while visiting family members both at home and abroad. These are very time-consuming duties, especially for a man in his 90s with multiple wives, 20 children, and a multitude of grandchildren and great-grandchildren.

Even after retirement, he remained dedicated to community service and his love for nature. Alongside his retired colleagues, he initiated the Retired Police and Tree Planters Association. Recognizing the need for meaningful activities and camaraderie among retired police officers, they chose tree planting as a way to stay engaged and make a positive impact. This endeavor not only keeps them busy but also fosters mutual support and the sharing of valuable information as they navigate their golden years.

My father valued education greatly and ensured it remained a top priority for all of us. He often assisted us with our homework and made a point of attending our school events and graduations. Despite being able to afford professional barber services, he chose to cut our hair himself with a simple hair clipper. I recall one instance when a colleague questioned why he didn't take us to a barber shop instead. He explained that these moments provided precious opportunities to bond with his children and impart wisdom in an informal setting. While he may not have been a skilled barber, he cherished such moments and the meaningful conversations they facilitated. I have followed in his footsteps by cutting my children's hair myself, using those moments to bond with my boys.

My father's first wife, Mami Christina, passed away during childbirth in 1965, before I was born. Although I never had the chance to know her, from what I've heard, she was a beautiful and kind-hearted wife and mother of three. After her passing, my father married my mother, who has always been the center of my world in many ways. She gave birth to ten children and showered me with love and attention. My mother worked tirelessly to shield my siblings and me from the challenges of growing up and competing for attention and resources.

My father's third wife, Mami Ceci, bore seven wonderful children. She is a shrewd businesswoman and a devout Christian in the Presbyterian Church. She has held various leadership roles in both her church and the community. She has a passion for travel, exploring both within Cameroon and internationally to visit her children and grandchildren.

CHAPTER 3

Mom and Siblings

*"A mother is like a kernel, crushed by problems but strong
enough to overcome them."*
—*African Proverb*

My mother, Magdalin, is part of an intriguing twin duo alongside her identical twin sister, Mary. Their striking resemblance often led to confusion among their spouses and children, especially when they dressed alike. Interestingly, while my mother has a set of twins among her 10 children, her sister has three sets of twins.

Standing at about 5 feet tall with a light complexion, my mother is undeniably beautiful. She is a deeply devout Catholic Christian, finding joy in singing in her church choir, participating in women's community groups, and visiting her grandchildren scattered across the globe. With a fondness for relating everything to the Bible, she often begins her conversations with us by quoting scripture: "The Bible says...," much to the amusement of my sisters and me.

Her upbringing was conventional for the time, as she was raised by her aunt rather than her biological parents. Fortunately, her aunt was wealthy during her days. Growing up in a privileged environment, she enjoyed activities like swimming and fishing with her cousin and girlfriends. After my father's first wife passed away, he was introduced to my mother, and they underwent a traditional marriage ceremony shortly thereafter. In those times, a simple visit to the bride's parents, accompanied by ceremonial palm wine, was sufficient to sanctify the marriage. However, it wasn't until several years later that my father legally married both my mother and his third wife, Mami Cecilia, in a courthouse ceremony.

According to my mother's account, my father came home for lunch one day and asked his two wives to dress up for a trip to the courthouse. Upon their arrival, they found a small gathering of friends and family waiting. The judge arrived with his assistants and spoke with my father for a few minutes, after which the court assistants brought some documents for his wives and the witnesses to sign. They signed without reading the contents. The whole process took about an hour. My mother said it wasn't until they got home that they pressed my father to tell them what they had signed. He revealed that it was their marriage certificate. They laughed at the fact that they had signed the documents without knowing what they were signing. They then asked my father for some money to go celebrate with their friends, which he happily obliged.

I seldom saw my mother angry, but sadness seemed to visit her more frequently, especially during our younger years. Even though I inquired about the cause of her sadness, she chose not to provide a direct response. Nowadays, she confides in me that, during those times, her sadness stemmed from the uncertainty of whether we, her young children, would grow into capable adults.

As my father's job required him to relocate every two years, he devised a plan to save money and prepare for retirement. He decided to alternate the company of his wives and their children every two years, with one wife accompanying him to his new posting while the other stayed in the village. This arrangement worked smoothly at first, but over time, the rotation schedule became complex for reasons that remain unclear to me even now.

During one of the periods when I resided in the village with my mother and siblings, I sensed that we were encountering financial difficulties, and it was then that I witnessed my mother's sadness. Despite this, I've never found the courage to discuss those days with my father. Strangely, it was during these times that I began to question and comprehend the world around me.

Reflecting on it now, my father's journey from poverty to success, owning multiple properties in different cities, seems like a paradox. Yet, his decision to split his family's residence between urban and rural areas sometimes left us grappling with financial challenges. This led me to question the concept of polygamy, the career that separated my family, the societal norms that condoned such practices, and, most significantly at the time, I questioned the God my mother spoke of as all-knowing and omnipresent.

My twin sister, Grace, is also very light-skinned like my mother and stands about 6 feet tall. Like me, she attended private boarding schools. She has always been very elegant and pretty. As a child, she had green eyes, as if she were wearing designer contacts, and a beautiful set of hair.

My mother describes Grace as always being quiet and observant, in contrast to her twin brother (yours truly), who would cry for hours and consume two and a half bottles of milk at each feeding. Grace had already started walking by about 10 months, while I was still crawling, talking, crying, and eating way more than she did. My mother said she often wondered if I would ever be able to walk. However, one morning, she asked Grace if she could teach me how to walk. Without hesitation, Grace came over and took my hand, leading me into the future. That's when I took my first step, and many more followed.

Grace and I followed our older half-brother, Peter, everywhere. Peter and I were very protective of our sister. We would get in trouble for "taking her" places around the neighborhood. I don't know if my sister liked school very much, but she did okay. She never complained about anything, so it was hard to tell. Since we went to different private boarding schools, we would only see each other during the breaks. I particularly enjoyed the summer breaks because we would be together with the rest of my siblings. My father loved farming, so we would drive to the farm, do some farming, and plant crops like corn, peanuts, beans, cassava, and yams, as well as eucalyptus trees, during those holidays.

A strange dynamic in my culture, which I think affected me, was that it was perfectly normal for children of one family member to live with other family members for several years. My mother had ten children: three boys and seven girls. My two older brothers, Andre and Victor, grew up with my uncles in two different cities, so I grew up not knowing them or being able to look up to them for guidance, protection, or any type of coaching that one gets from an older brother. I wanted to learn from them how to talk to girls, how to dress, what kinds of risks to take, what kinds of fights to get into, and when to walk away. In short, I didn't get the benefit of their advice. However, I enjoyed the attention I got from my sisters, my mother, and my beloved grandmother, Anna Tangwi. But I would've loved to have my father and older brothers around all the time. For the most part, Andre and Victor always seemed like strangers in my life, no matter how hard I tried to get close to them. I barely knew them, and I still have not been able to spend much time with them since we now live thousands of miles apart.

Most of the pre-puberty experiences and other street skills I learned came from my childhood friend Wilson, who lived across the street from us. Wilson and I were inseparable when I wasn't with Peter and Grace. Wilson grew up with a single father after his mother left. He was very street-smart and generous with his knowledge. He taught me how to swim, bike, and talk to girls. He always stressed the importance of dressing well and looking good. We spent a great deal of time together during our teenage years, until we went to different high schools and, subsequently, different universities. Wilson was one of those people in my life with whom I shared a secret language that only the two of us understood. He lived in Oklahoma City for a few years before being repatriated to Cameroon in 2006. Unfortunately, Wilson passed away in Bamenda in 2019 from health complications.

It wasn't just my brothers, Andre and Victor, who were absent during my impressionable years; my older half-brother Ben also left to study in the United States when I was only

6 years old. My entire family has been, and continues to be, blessed by Ben, my father's first child and a selfless man. Ni Ben, as we respectfully refer to him, is the angel that every family would love to have. Although I didn't know him very well at the time, I knew he was heading far away when he left for the United States. He later told me that he saw his first television set in Paris while in transit to the U.S. and the first computer when he arrived at the University of Wisconsin-Stevens Point (UWSP). Despite what might have been a late start with modern technology, he worked hard and made good grades. He later moved to Springfield, Illinois, to attend graduate school. During this time, my brother sent money home to help my father pay for our school fees. As a result, my father was able to send all of us to really good schools. Most of us attended private boarding schools and were the envy of the village. My brother's hard work and sacrifice made it possible for most of my siblings to attend secondary school and universities.

CHAPTER 4

Boy to Man

"The young can walk faster, but the elder knows the road."
—*African Proverb*

I attended mostly private boarding schools, where I matured from a boy into a man. It was there that I developed most of my critical thinking and leadership skills. Some of my best and worst memories occurred during my time at these boarding schools.

Set in a lush, green landscape in my hometown, Bali Nyonga, the Cameroon Protestant College (CPC) boasts a serene and expansive campus and provides an ideal atmosphere for learning, reflection, and personal growth. Blending historic charm with modern infrastructure, the school offers a well-rounded environment for academic and extracurricular growth. The campus features equipped classroom blocks and laboratories, fostering hands-on learning in science, arts, and technical subjects. Students also benefit from a resourceful library, a chapel for spiritual growth, and sports facilities for football, volleyball, and track and field.

By balancing tradition with modern education, CPC Bali fosters a strong sense of community, discipline, and excellence among its students. As a boarding school, CPC Bali provides dormitories that promote discipline and community living. My first week at boarding school in 1988 was a mix of happiness, excitement, uncertainty, and fear. The fear stemmed primarily from the strange induction rituals that boarding students at the time underwent, which involved whipping the younger students, collecting money from them, forcing them to clean shoes, and even eating fish or meat from their food plates. I'm not sure if the school authorities were aware of the extent of what was going on.

Our dormitories were named after prominent figures in our school's history. Each house contained about six rooms and housed seven to ten boys. The older students slept in single beds or in the lower bunks. These older students were both our tormentors and mentors. They made us do crazy things for their amusement, but also looked out for us, ensuring that students from other houses didn't mistreat us. It was a strange relationship, but it made perfect sense to me at the time. I was in "Fonyonga House," named after the second king of the Bali Nyonga kingdom, Fonyonga II. Our dormitory was Dorm 15, and as a freshman, I slept on the upper bunk.

Schoolwork was rigorous, and the expectations were very high. I did okay academically at first, but later I became interested in things other than schoolwork. I enjoyed and excelled in literature and history, but I hated math with a passion. This dislike impacted my understanding of physics, biology, and chemistry once those subjects required calculations. I eventually transferred to other boarding schools where I made friends, started dating, and even began drinking beer. I never smoked because I hated the smell. Once, I asked one of my cousins, nicknamed Ndolo, who smoked, if I could "try it" to see what it tasted like. He told me I should wait until I was ready to smoke full-time, and if I didn't want to smoke full-time, it didn't matter what it tasted like. I think that moment stuck with me and kept me away from smoking.

When I graduated from high school in 1997, I had the option of attending one of three universities that offered Law and Political Science: the University of Buea, which followed the Anglo-Saxon educational system; the University of Yaoundé II; or the University of Dschang. Both Yaoundé II and Dschang were predominantly run under the French system, with most classes taught in French.

I graduated from high school alongside my cousin Roland, who had lived with my family during his high school years. My father said it would be more expensive for both of us to attend different universities, as we would need two separate apartments and would incur two sets of expenses. Roland wanted to study Business, Economics, and Accounting, and at the time, the University of Dschang seemed to have a more established program compared to the English-speaking University of Buea, which was relatively new.

I decided that we should both attend the French-speaking University of Dschang and share a room to ease the financial burden and enable Roland to attend university. However, that arrangement only lasted a few semesters, as we ended up getting separate apartments anyway.

I pursued a double major in Law and Political Science, but encountered challenges studying in French. Hailing from the English-speaking region of Cameroon, I had English as my primary language of learning. Unfortunately, the educational structure at the University of Dschang did not adequately accommodate English-speaking students like myself. As a result, attending classes became increasingly disheartening, and the mounting pressure to excel academically and secure a successful future weighed heavily on me.

Amid these challenges, I met a girl named Zoless and fell deeply in love with her. One afternoon after school, my best friend, Liese, and I were walking to my apartment when we spotted an elegant, slender, light-skinned girl. As we approached, Liese recognized her immediately as someone we had attended high school with. He called out, "Zoless!" and she recognized both of us. After chatting on the street for about twenty minutes, I impulsively invited her to join us at an outdoor concert happening later that evening, and she agreed.

That night, I couldn't take my eyes off her. The band playing was one of my favorites: *Petit Pays et les Sans Visa.* We enjoyed their latest tunes while my friend and I had beer, and Zoless opted for soda and water. When the event ended past 3 a.m., we couldn't find a taxi to her place, so we walked two miles to her apartment. Along the way, our conversation ranged from high school memories to university life and the challenges of the French education system. We also laughed about memorable moments from the concert. At her apartment, I expressed my desire to see her again, and she warmly agreed. Though I didn't get a kiss that night, the promise of future meetings was the perfect ending to a wonderful evening.

Following that night, Zoless and I grew closer, spending increasingly more time together. My aspiration to become a lawyer stemmed from a genuine interest in the law and my father's desire for one of his children to pursue legal studies. Initially, I dreamed of leveraging legal expertise to enter politics, even aspiring to run for president someday. However, my academic performance fell short of expectations, dimming these prospects. Instead, I found myself channeling my energy into my relationship with Zoless. Despite having two apartments available, Zoless's place became our primary sanctuary, with my flat serving merely as a stopover when we were in that part of town.

We seized every opportunity during breaks and holidays to travel across the country, visiting friends and family. Our university, like most in Cameroon, experienced frequent student protests and strikes. During one such strike, Zoless and I decided to escape to the capital city of Yaoundé. While I visited my elder brother Andre, and Zoless visited her uncle, we remained close, spending significant time together in the city. We met almost daily. One particular night, after saying goodbye to Zoless, I returned home to find Andre on the phone with my twin sister Grace, who had relocated to the United States to live with our eldest half-brother, Ni Ben. When I asked to speak with her, I confided in her about my challenges at university. She encouraged me to seek Ni Ben's guidance and passed him the phone. That conversation changed the course of my life.

CHAPTER 5

The Phone Call

"Never throw your reserved water, simply because you heard it will be raining."
—African Proverb

My brother Ni Ben came on the line and said, "Sama," (calling me by my middle name), "how are you doing? I have been reading on the internet about the student protests at your university. Are you okay?" He sounded like my dad, with urgency and concern in his voice.

"Hello, Ni Ben, we are ok, thank you for asking. The protests have been going on for a couple of weeks now. However, I am in Yaoundé to get away from it all," I replied.

"That's okay. Do you think you will be able to go back and finish your law degree?"

"I don't think so, I'm way behind now," I said, feeling a bit ashamed.

"I contacted the registrar at the University of Illinois Urbana-Champaign," he said calmly, "and he said if you have your degree in Cameroon, you can do a full year at their university and get a degree from Urbana-Champaign. He also said that it would allow you to go to law school here in America."

"That would be nice," I said, "but I am thinking of doing something else. Something in sociology that would allow me to do youth programming or work with the elderly." Ni Ben didn't say anything right away. He had been taken aback by my answer, I think.

"I thought you always wanted to be a lawyer," he said. I was quiet, not quite sure what to say.

"In any case," he continued, "you can still go to law school after your sociology degree if you want to." That sounded much better. I was on board with that idea.

"Great," I said, happy with what he said. "What do I have to do now to get admission in a US university?"

"I will mail an application form from the University of Wisconsin-Stevens Point for you to fill out," he said. "Attach your high school transcript and mail them back to the school. I will be notified once they receive your documents. UWSP is a great school, and I think you will like it there."

I didn't know what to say. In the space of a few minutes and a few words, Ni Ben was about to change the course of my life. But I blurted almost in a whisper, "Thank you, Ni Ben!"

"You're welcome," he replied with an obvious smile in his voice. "Stay well and take care," he added before hanging up.

When the line went dead, I was still clutching the cell phone to my ear. I could not believe what had just happened and could not wait to tell my girlfriend the good news the following day. It was a long night as I tossed and turned in bed, thinking of my life in America.

Under Ni Ben's guidance, I navigated to the school's website to access the online application form instead of waiting weeks for a mailed copy. After several days, I successfully downloaded the form and obtained copies of both my high school and university transcripts. With meticulous care, I completed the application, compiled all necessary documents, and headed to the post office. There, I sent off the package containing my application materials to the University of Wisconsin-Stevens Point, eagerly awaiting the next chapter of my journey.

As I left the post office, a curious sensation of relief washed over me, its origins elusive yet undeniable. Perhaps it stemmed from the seamless assembly and mailing of the complete package, a task accomplished with unexpected ease. Or maybe it was the realization that I had taken that crucial first concrete step toward shaping my future. Whatever the reason, a weight had been lifted, and a sense of anticipation for what lay ahead began to settle in.

I went to an internet café and bought 30 minutes of airtime to email Ni Ben. It took about 19 minutes for the page to load before I could type my message. I wrote a few lines to let him know I had mailed the package and to thank him for the opportunity. It took another five minutes for the mail to be "sent." I used the remaining six minutes to explore the university's website. I could not read past a few pages because the internet was so slow, but at least what I learned made me even more excited about the school and my journey to America.

I went back to the internet café several more times and looked at other schools in the US. I realized I could also apply to other schools online, so I decided to apply to three other colleges just for fun. I eventually received responses from all four schools, but three of them sent form letters that seemed to be template correspondences.

Receiving the letter from UWSP was a momentous occasion, made even more special by the handwritten note from Dr. Fang Marcus, the director of the Foreign Student Office. As I read Dr. Fang's message, a deep sense of connection and warmth enveloped me, solidifying my desire to attend this university. The day I received my acceptance letter and Form I-20, signifying my admission to UWSP, felt like a triumph akin to winning the lottery.

Returning to the village to assist my mother with farm duties and any other tasks she required, I brought along my acceptance letter to share the news with my father. He was very happy and proud of me, and we began making plans for me to return to Yaoundé, the capital, to initiate my visa application. However, before proceeding, I needed to secure a bank statement to demonstrate that my family could financially support my studies in America. A crucial component of the visa application requirements, the bank statement would substantiate our ability to cover out-of-state tuition fees, living expenses, and health insurance costs.

Accompanied by my father, I embarked on a journey to Douala, Cameroon's economic hub, to obtain a bank statement. During our travels, my father shared with me invaluable advice from his aunt, Mami Anna Ndi (of blessed memory), who had encouraged him to open a savings account from an early age. It was through this foresight and financial prudence that my father was able to demonstrate his ability to support my education in the United States. With careful planning, he ensured the account held sufficient funds to meet the consular officer's requirements, thereby assuring my financial stability abroad.

CHAPTER 6

The Visa Interview in Yaoundé

"The stone in the river does not fear the rain."
—*African Proverb*

Armed with the crucial bank statement, I made my way to Yaoundé while my father returned to our hometown. In the capital city, I rendezvoused with my sister, Ma Kah Rosemary, at my brother, Andre's, residence. Our time together was truly unforgettable. My sister possessed a gentle demeanor, marked by her soft-spoken nature and innate ability to solve problems. She was unwavering in her support for her siblings, always ready to stand up for them at a moment's notice. Despite her nursing qualifications, securing a government job in Cameroon proved challenging due to limited opportunities and widespread corruption within the system. Refusing to compromise her principles, my sister opted to work as a private nurse at various clinics, dedicating significant time to caring for those in need, particularly in rural areas. Additionally, she engaged in entrepreneurial ventures, buying and selling goods to supplement her income. Her resilience and compassion were evident in her commitment to her profession, family, and community.

Over the next several days, as I waited for my interview date, my sister Ma Kah and I practiced sample questions and scenarios that I would have to answer to obtain a visa. My brother, Ni Ben, also sent some sample questions and coached me on what to expect during the interview. On the day of the interview, we rose early, and Andre kindly offered to drop us off at the embassy before heading to work. The imposing structure of the US Embassy loomed before us, but painfully, there were no seating arrangements for those awaiting their turn outside. Braving the sweltering heat, we waited patiently under the sun's unforgiving rays until my name was finally called. Ma Kah hugged me and wished me luck as the security officer pointed toward the main entrance, where I was given a number. I joined a group of well-dressed students, all looking very serious, nervous, and, in a strange way, excited. As we queued up to enter the interview hall, I exchanged a shy smile with the girl ahead of me, who was focused on her number slip. Taking her cue, I glanced at my slip to double-check my assigned number. It read: number 9.

We were led into a room adorned with a bench against one wall, directly facing a glass partition with small windows carved into it. Through these windows, we could catch glimpses of the consulate officers bustling about. Desks were scattered across the vast space behind the glass, with officers engaged in various tasks: some typing away on computers, others conversing over the phone, and a few moving between desks. Despite the apparent busyness, a palpable sense of contentment filled the room, evident in the officers' demeanor as they carried out their duties. Bright lighting illuminated the space, and several fans lazily spun from the high ceilings, offering a stark contrast to the heat outside.

Dressed in a light pink short-sleeved button-down shirt, black trousers, and dark brown leather shoes, I felt confident and poised as I waited for my turn with the interviewer. The consulate officer called out the first candidate's name, prompting my heart to quicken. Stepping up to the glass window, the candidate faced the officer, who maintained a stern and professional demeanor. With measured precision, the officer posed a series of questions before the candidate produced a folder containing documents, which he handed over for review. Silently, the officer meticulously examined each page before abruptly reaching for a stamp, pressing it twice onto an ink pad, and imprinting it onto the document before him. With a solemn tone, the officer informed the young man that his application had been denied.

Observing the applicant's body language, I noticed his shoulders slump, though I couldn't discern his facial expression. With a gesture of disbelief, he reached up to wipe his face with his right hand, seemingly stunned by the outcome. Rendered speechless, he did not attempt to respond as the officer returned his documents. With trembling hands, he accepted the papers, turning away almost in slow motion. His face appeared pale, and a profound sadness hung about him as he retreated from the window.

Empathizing with the rejected applicant, I couldn't help but feel a bit of sorrow for him and wished I could hug him to make him feel better. Strangely, though, I thought his failure would increase my chances of getting a visa, since rumor had it that there was a daily visa quota. The next candidate was also called by name. I assumed she had the number two ticket. She was wearing a red dress and had this confident look about her. She stepped up to the window without hesitation and handed her documents to the officer unprompted. The officer made small talk with her as he perused her documents. Then he asked without preamble: "Why do you want to go to America?"

She was quiet for a few moments as if she had not thought about that before. Then she mumbled something to the officer, which I could not hear clearly. He asked her a couple more questions, but she seemed to struggle with her answers and kept her voice low. I saw the officer grab the stamp again and stamped one of the documents, then told her that her application had been denied. Her shoulders sank as she turned around to leave. With a heavy heart, she turned away, shoulders slumped in defeat, before hastily gathering her papers and bidding farewell to the rest of us with a faint wave. A wave of emotion seemed to engulf her as she made her way toward the exit, her demeanor hinting at the brink of tears. Again, I felt sorry for her, but selfishly thought of my odds too. The consular officer's seat at the window remained empty for about five minutes.

During this time, we sat in subdued silence, anticipation hanging thick in the air, each of us anxiously awaiting the next summons. I couldn't help but feel sorry for the individual holding the number three ticket, likely feeling the weight of the moment. Taking a moment to collect my thoughts, I rifled through my folder, mentally retracing the organization of my documents. Ensuring everything was in order, I reviewed the contents, beginning with a copy of my application to UWSP for reference, followed by my financial documents, including my father's bank statement, as well as my acceptance letter, Form I-20, and family photos to bolster my case. Additionally, I had gathered supplementary materials from the web about the University of Wisconsin–Stevens Point and the broader UW System to provide comprehensive support for my application.

Caught off guard by the unexpected call of my name, "Samuel Sama Dinga," I felt a surge of adrenaline flood my veins. Despite holding ticket number nine and anticipating a later summons, I was suddenly thrust into the spotlight. A dryness settled in my mouth, and my heart thundered so loudly that I feared it echoed throughout the room. I glanced at the rest of the candidates sitting on the bench as if to seek their confirmation that it was my name that had been called. With a gulp, I swallowed the lump in my throat, drawing in a deep breath to steady my nerves. Stepping forward, I approached the small glass window, mustering the courage to greet the officer with a tentative "Good morning." His nod in response offered a semblance of encouragement as I braced myself for the impending interview. He then asked me how I was doing. I told him I was a little nervous but okay. He smiled, and I was relieved that the officer's initial demeanor was welcoming.

I handed over one set of documents, retaining the copies for reference. With a practiced hand, he meticulously sifted through the folder's contents, scrutinizing each document. Anticipating the inevitable question about my motivations for studying in America, I braced myself for the customary "Why do you want to study in America?" Instead, to my surprise, the officer posed a different question: "What do you know about the University of Wisconsin–Stevens Point?" A gentle smile played across my lips, conveying a hint of confidence as if to say that was easy. I told him about all the knowledge I had been reading online about the university – not only about UWSP but also about the UW System. He seemed to be taking notes as I poured it out, but I could not see what he was writing.

"What do you want to study and why?" he then asked.

"I'd like to study Sociology, in particular the programs that will deal with either youth programming or any program related to adult life and aging."

He halted his writing and lifted his gaze. I was confused by the move because I could not immediately tell whether I had said the wrong thing. Sensing an opportunity to elaborate, I shared a personal anecdote about my family's extensive lineage, tracing back to my grandfather, who had over 80 wives and countless descendants. With earnest sincerity, I expressed my aspiration to study Sociology, explaining my desire to utilize this knowledge to serve my vast family network. Whether through youth programming initiatives or by developing programs to assist the elderly in my family and community, I emphasized my commitment to leveraging my education to benefit my family and my country of Cameroon.

He started jotting notes again as I spoke, smiling in a way that told me he was fascinated by my personal story. I looked in my folder and produced a picture of my family. His jaw dropped in amazement. The photo showed my grandfather's many wives and children, all of them half-naked as was the dressing at the time, taken after the passing of my grandfather. After examining the photo intently for a minute, the consular officer asked for permission to share it with his colleagues, which I readily granted. He hurried to the back of the room, beckoning his colleagues to join him. I watched him converse with them, likely recounting the details I had shared about my family. Their collective attention shifted between me and the photo as they absorbed the story.

During this brief interlude, a wave of apprehension washed over me as I pondered the implications of sharing the photo. However, before I could dwell on it, the officer returned with a beaming smile. After thanking me for letting him share the photo, he asked about my financial documents to support my stay in the United States. I directed him to the bank statement page. He studied it carefully, then reached for the phone, made a call, and gave the bank account number to whoever was on the line. He listened for a while, then thanked the person and hung up. He wrote some more notes and then looked up.

"Congratulations, Mr. Dinga, we will grant you a visa to study at the University of Wisconsin." He probably said more, but I heard nothing else after those first few words. I stood in shock and disbelief as the consular officer took a postcard-sized paper, checked a few boxes on the side, grabbed a different stamp, stamped the card, and signed it.

"Go over to the next room to pay your visa fee and then return on Thursday after 3:00 p.m. to pick up your visa. Good luck with your studies!"

"Thank you, Sir!" I said as I gathered my remaining documents. As I turned to leave, I was met with a sea of smiling faces, beaming with pride at my breaking the morning's streak of refusals. I returned their smiles with a thumbs-up and an affirming nod, then headed to the next room to complete the visa payment.

As I emerged from the embassy, I searched for my sister, Ma Kah, who had been waiting patiently for my return.

Despite my overwhelming happiness, I restrained my excitement, mindful of others who might have faced disappointment. Sensing my subdued demeanor, Ma Kah instinctively moved closer, intertwining her fingers with mine as we walked in silence toward a taxi waiting down the street.

Once inside the taxi, I handed her the card indicating my visa approval. With a glance at it, she turned to me, her eyes widening in disbelief. Without a word, she enveloped me in a tight embrace, a silent exchange of joy and relief passing between us. Throughout the rest of the journey, neither of us spoke of the interview or the visa, content to bask in the shared moment of triumph and gratitude.

With my passport and visa secured, my brother, Ben, wasted no time arranging my flight itinerary. To streamline the process and avoid time constraints, he advised against traveling back to the village to bid farewell to our relatives. Instead, he directed me to head straight to Douala, where I would embark on my journey with Air France, connecting via Paris. The flight was scheduled for Saturday, January 10th, 2002, marking the beginning of my adventure abroad.

My girlfriend, Zoless, had plans to travel to Bamenda for her cousin's wedding, and I hoped to meet her after I collected my visa. However, our plans were disrupted when Ni Ben insisted I head directly to Douala without returning to Bamenda. With cell phones not yet widely used, I couldn't inform Zoless of the change in plans. After leaving Yaoundé, I traveled to Douala, where I confirmed my Air France flight. I then stayed at my aunt's house for a few days, joined by family members. We shared a pleasant lunch on my final day, during which many offered counsel and words of wisdom for my upcoming journey.

One piece of advice that resonated with me came from my cousin, Titus Fomusoh (RIP), who had lived in the United States before.

"You're heading to a place with bustling streets and fast-moving traffic," he said. "Make sure to act with purpose and decisiveness, or you might miss your exit. If you miss your exit, you cannot just turn around or reverse. You need to drive to the next exit, and if you're not lucky, it could be several miles out. This will cost you time and money and might get you lost altogether."

It took me several years to understand what my cousin meant by his analogy: he was talking about all the opportunities in America. He was cautioning me to consider my options carefully and be deliberate with my decisions, so I wouldn't choose the wrong path that might take a while to correct.

At my send-off party, my brother Ben's close friend, Mola Eric Tande, who was visiting from Chicago, shared valuable insights about America, specifically UWSP, as he is an alumnus of the university. He emphasized the importance of paying attention during orientation, where administrators would provide essential information for my journey at UWSP. Grateful for his advice, I expressed my determination to excel, promising to surpass the achievements of both Ben and Eric and set new benchmarks. Eric beamed with pride, capturing the moment on tape as we shared in the excitement of the upcoming adventure.

As we embarked on the journey to the airport in an 18-passenger van, a bittersweet feeling washed over me as I glanced at my loved ones' faces. Tears welled up in my eyes as I grappled with the uncertainty of whether I would ever see some of them again. Despite the emotional turmoil, my family filled the van with songs of praise and gratitude, thanking God and our ancestors for the opportunity to study abroad. It was a moment of mixed emotions, filled with both sadness at the prospect of parting and joy for the blessings bestowed upon me.

The airport was crowded, hot, loud, and chaotic. My father joined us with a couple of his friends. His presence filled me with happiness, and I was overjoyed to see him. As the time for departure drew near, I embraced each of my loved ones tightly, tears streaming down my face as I struggled to say goodbye. The pain of leaving behind those closest to me weighed heavily on my heart; each farewell hug was accompanied by a flood of emotions.

In a tender moment with my sister Ma Kah, she imparted words of wisdom, whispering in my ear, "Work hard, continue to help others, and change the world." Her heartfelt encouragement moved me deeply, prompting more tears to flow. With a heavy heart, I followed my father through the maze of security checkpoints toward the awaiting aircraft. His position in the police force afforded us the privilege of bypassing the usual procedures, allowing him to accompany me directly to the gates and onto the plane. My father glanced at my ticket and showed me where I was supposed to sit. Then he handed me an envelope for my brother, Ben. He hugged me and said, "Make me proud in America!"

CHAPTER 7

America—Here I Come

"You can never cross the ocean until you dare to lose sight of the shore."
—*African Proverb*

I had been on planes before this trip. As a police commissioner, my father had travel vouchers that allowed us to fly within Cameroon for vacation. As we grew older and my parents had more children, we switched to road trips in a 504 Peugeot or whatever car my father owned at the time. Now, sitting in the huge Air France 747, my mind was lost in thought and anxiety. From my middle seat, I couldn't look out the window or easily access the aisle for stretching or restroom visits, but that was the least of my worries.

A man occupied the aisle seat, and two women sat to my right. The women were elegantly dressed and their hair beautifully styled. They appeared to know each other and had likely made this trip before, talking and laughing carefree. The man to my left was casually dressed and seemed to want solitude, perhaps hoping to nap or was just simply bored. After fastening my seatbelt, I tried to familiarize myself with my surroundings. I attempted to greet my neighbors, who either didn't hear me or were uninterested in who sat beside them. I looked around in astonishment at the sea of people on the airplane, my mind preoccupied with questions about their destinations and purposes. Some must have been returning home; others were students like myself; some were traveling for business, and others for leisure; I wished I could interview them all.

It took about two hours for everyone to settle into their seats. The flight attendants bustled up and down the aisle, counting and recounting passengers, writing on their clipboards and conferring as if solving a puzzle. They ensured the overhead compartments were properly secured, seat belts were fastened, and excess bags were stored under seats. Over the speakers, the lead flight attendant introduced herself and spoke for about three minutes, providing instructions and reviewing rules. He emphasized that smoking was forbidden and disruptive passengers would be reported to authorities, delivering the message in both English and French.

Then a different voice came over the intercom as flight attendants lined the aisles with safety equipment. They demonstrated safety procedures as the voice explained them. Finally, a male voice announced, "Good evening, ladies and gentlemen, this is your captain speaking..." He spoke with authority, sharing the flight duration and weather conditions before thanking us for choosing Air France. He concluded by encouraging us to sit back, relax, and enjoy the flight.

The plane slowly backed up, surged forward, and the captain announced we were fourth in line and would depart soon. Flight attendants continued patrolling the aisles as the plane rolled forward. The aircraft stopped, and I heard the powerful engines idling on the tarmac. The pilot then addressed the crew: "Flight attendants, prepare for takeoff." All flight attendants took their seats and fastened their seatbelts like the passengers.

After about five minutes, without warning, the plane surged forward and gained speed. I felt the nose lift as it continued to thrust forward. Then the entire aircraft lifted, and we were airborne. Looking ahead, it seemed like we were climbing a steep hill, a position the plane maintained for about two to three minutes. The massive aircraft swayed right, then left, as it continued to ascend. The cabin was quiet except for a few passengers, including the two women next to me who kept talking and laughing.

As the plane leveled off, the pilot announced excellent weather conditions. He reported cruising at 472 miles per hour at 27,000 feet, with an intended cruising altitude of 37,000 feet. About twenty minutes later, a chime sounded. The pilot announced we had reached our cruising altitude of 37,000 feet and again encouraged us to enjoy the flight.

The flight crew resumed their duties, pushing drink carts from the front of the plane. It took a while for them to reach us, in what I later learned was the economy section. I didn't know that food and drinks were included in my ticket price, so I cautiously ordered a Heineken and a bottle of water. My father had given me 10,000 francs (about $20) as he walked me to the plane, and I was certain that would cover a drink and a meal. A couple of hours later, the crew returned with food carts. They announced the meal choices, and since I didn't know the options, I accepted their last suggestion, chicken with tomato sauce, couscous, salad, and bread. They offered more drinks, which I accepted despite worrying about exceeding my budget. I noticed everyone accepting second drinks without paying. I enjoyed my meal with a second cold Heineken, momentarily forgetting my anxiety about flying.

The flight attendants collected our empty trays and accumulated garbage. At this point, it struck me that I was being served by white people; significant because I had only seen white people being served by Black people in movies and at local establishments like the Police Canteen, the Senior Service Club, and the Atlantic Beach Hotel in Limbe, Cameroon. This role reversal reminded me of my father's words: "Whether you are white or black, we all have our place, roles, duties and responsibilities." For that brief moment, being served by white people made me feel important and wealthy.

The crew came around again offering drinks, but this time I worried about deportation for failing to pay my food and drink bill. I asked the flight attendant how much I had accumulated. She looked confused, glancing around as if I were speaking to someone else or needed help from a colleague. As I started to clarify, understanding dawned on her face, and she explained with a slight grin that all meals and drinks were included in my ticket price. Relieved by this news, I ordered another Heineken, which tasted even better now that I knew I wouldn't have to pay extra.

After the meal, I watched a movie playing on the common screen suspended from the cabin ceiling. The cabin lights dimmed, and eventually, I dozed off for about four hours.

A light tap on my shoulder startled me awake. A flight attendant was distributing warm, wet towels. Initially unsure of their purpose, I glanced around the cabin and realized they were meant to refresh our faces. I smiled as I joined the other passengers in this ritual. The carts appeared again, this time with breakfast: croissants, orange juice, and a choice of tea or coffee. Everything tasted better without the worry of cost. After about an hour, the pilot announced our approach to Paris-Charles de Gaulle Airport. As the plane descended, I experienced an intense pressure in my ears, a sensation I'd never felt before and that no one had warned me about. About thirty-five minutes later, the plane made its final approach and touched down with a screech. I felt the wheels rolling on the tarmac as the aircraft taxied to its gate. The pilot welcomed us to Paris, announcing the temperature as 1°C and local time as 6:45 a.m. He thanked us for flying Air France and wished safe onward journeys to connecting passengers. I appreciated the exceptional service from both the flight crew and the pilot.

The reality of the weather sank in as we gathered our bags to depart. My uncle had bought me a pre-owned winter coat in Cameroon. I put it on, feeling Parisian until the cold air hit my face. My lips dried instantly, and the brutal cold stung my skin. As I descended the stairs to the waiting bus, my eyes felt dry, and my body shivered. My fingers were so numb I could barely grip my hand luggage. I wanted to run, but everyone else remained calm, orderly, and almost nonchalant about the cold. I tried to match their composure as the frigid air ripped through my lungs with each breath. I wore thin-soled shoes that had been fashionable and suitable for Cameroon's warm weather. When I stepped onto the tarmac, my feet felt like popsicles on a hockey rink. Every step sent pain shooting through my bones. My shins ached, and the distance to the bus seemed like a trek through the Alps.

I tried to swallow, but my throat felt constricted. My breath released vapor like cigarette smoke, and I noticed everyone else had the same clouds emerging from their mouths and noses as they breathed. Finally reaching the bus, I found a few empty seats while most passengers stood. Though slightly warmer inside, the open doors let frigid air stream in, chilling me further. I collapsed into an open seat, forgetting my mother's Christian teaching about offering seats to women, children, and the elderly.

The driver closed the doors and warned us to hold on, but warming up remained my only concern. We drove for about five minutes, weaving between cargo trucks, buses, and parked planes. The driver pulled up to one of the terminals and announced we should disembark. Though I dreaded stepping into the cold again, the bus stopped close to the building, requiring only five steps to reach the entrance. After another rigorous security check, we faced a five-hour layover before boarding our flight to the United States.

CHAPTER 8

Chicago O'Hare Airport

"No matter how far you are from your house, you will keep going until you get home."
—*African Proverb*

By the second flight to Chicago, I knew what to expect from these massive aircraft with hundreds of passengers. The flight was uneventful. I watched movies on my screen mounted in the seat ahead of me, had two more beers, and ate some unremarkable food. During the eight-hour flight, my window seat offered a perfect view of America as we approached. I marveled at Chicago's immensity and its well-planned houses and streets. The size and length of the interstate highways from above astounded me, and I wondered how it would feel to drive on them. As we descended toward the runway and touched down, we taxied to our gate. The pilot announced the temperature was 43°F and the local time was 3:15 p.m.

My fears about the cold returned, but fortunately, we remained indoors. We walked through a narrow jetway into an open hall filled with security personnel. This was after the

September 11 attacks in New York, when planes had been used as weapons against the United States, so security was stringent. As we walked quietly with our passports in hand, a lady approached with a German shepherd, and my heart sank. Let me explain my reaction. In Cameroon, people rarely keep dogs as pets. Most dog owners have them for security, and the animals are trained to attack intruders. I had always avoided dogs, so this officer with her German shepherd deeply unsettled me. I summoned all my courage and tried to remain calm. The dog seemed uninterested in me, merely sniffing my shoulder bag before moving on. My heart still raced from the encounter, and I missed the next officer's instructions. He had to tap me to indicate which line to join. I nodded and smiled awkwardly as I followed his direction. One by one, we were called to speak with immigration officers. When my turn came, the officer motioned me forward. I approached uncertainly, aware of rumors that entry to the United States could be denied for any reason, even at this point. I tried to smile, but my mouth was dry, and my ears hadn't adjusted from the plane's descent. Everything sounded as if I were in an echo chamber or a nightclub with deafening music.

The officer greeted me and reached for my passport and Form I-20, which showed that I was a foreign student. He studied the documents, grabbed a stamp, and said, "UW-Madison is a great school; my cousin went there." Without hesitation, I replied, "No, I'm going to UW-Stevens Point." He looked up, his face puzzled, and told me that my passport indicated UW-Madison and that he could not let me in just yet. My worst fears began to unfold before my eyes, but almost on cue, another officer, standing between two booths, turned, looked at my passport, and said they had seen a few cases like this. She explained further that UW-Madison was the most popular of the UW system schools. I felt hurt that my school-to-be was now second place, but that was not a battle I could fight at that moment. I realized that if this was the rationale that would get me through the gates of hope, then my school could be in 13th place for all I cared. The male officer, after listening to the female officer, whom I assumed was his superior, stamped my passport and said, "Welcome to America." I gave a huge sigh of relief under my breath and said, "Thank you, sir." He ushered me toward the baggage claim area, but since I had only my small bag, I proceeded to the exit, where the huge double doors swung open as if America were spreading its arms to welcome its newborn son.

CHAPTER 9

Family Reunion

"A person is a person because of other people."
—*Zulu Proverb*

Many people were waiting for family, friends, or customers. I scanned the crowd but couldn't spot my brother, Ben. I pushed forward, my anticipation growing, and then I saw the back of his head just before he turned around. He greeted me with a huge smile and opened his arms for a bear hug. At that moment, my twin sister, who had also been scanning the crowd, saw us and rushed over. She had a camera but completely forgot about it in her excitement to give me a long, tight hug as well. We exchanged a few words, and then my brother ushered us to a nearby corner to sit. Everything around me felt grand—the airport waiting room, the seats, the doors—everything seemed larger than I was used to.

We sat down, and they asked about our family back home and how my trip had gone. My sister, Grace, reached into her bag and pulled out a wrapped package of fried chicken that my brother's wife, Dr. Frida, had prepared for me. She also handed me a can of Mountain Dew, which I found too sweet. As we ate and chatted, I shared stories about my visa interview, the cold in Paris, and the food-and-drink debacle on the plane. They laughed so hard, and I felt so happy to see them. We stayed at the airport because I had a connecting flight to Wisconsin, where I was going to attend school. I told them I'd like to convert my 10,000 CFA francs (about $20) to US dollars. We went to an exchange kiosk, but the attendant told us that the amount was too small to exchange. I was shocked because this was considered a decent amount of money back home, where most families live on this for a month or more. I wasn't happy about this discovery, but I didn't have time to dwell on it. So, we hopped on the tram and headed to the terminal for my connecting flight to Central Wisconsin Airport.

At this point, I had given my brother, Ben, a letter from my dad. He read it quickly and tucked it away. I wasn't sure what was in the letter, but I could tell from his reaction that it didn't bring him much happiness. He put on a brave face, but I have a knack for reading people, even someone like him, whom I hadn't seen in a long time.

At the terminal, we spent about 30 minutes talking before it was time to check in and fly to my new home. My brother handed me a huge duffel bag, a real winter coat, and brown leather gloves. I tried them on, and they felt so warm and cozy. "This is what I needed in Paris," I told them as we hugged again.

I checked in my duffel bag and then headed to the small aircraft. This time, we also had to step outside and climb up to the plane, but I was prepared for the cold. I climbed aboard and peeked into the cramped cabin. I think there were fewer than 20 people on the small plane.

When the plane started taxiing, the pilot welcomed us and reminded us that we were on the flight to Central Wisconsin Airport (CWA). He encouraged us to keep our seat belts fastened at all times, as the flight would be rough due to snow and winds. Sure enough, the turbulence was scary, but as we left the Chicago airspace, it quieted down, and we had a smooth flight. It took less than an hour to land at CWA.

I headed to baggage claim to grab my duffel bag when I saw a young Japanese man holding up a sign with my name. I walked up to him and said, "I'm Sam Dinga." He smiled, and we shook hands. He introduced himself as Ben from the International Programs Office at UWSP.

At that moment, I was confused because I didn't know that Japanese people had "English" names. I told him that my brother's name was also Ben.

"Oh, cool," he said.

As we were heading out of the airport, I saw a Black man walking toward me, also smiling. I smiled back as he approached.

"Are you Sam?" he inquired.

"Yes," I answered.

"My name is Professor Ben, and your cousin Evans asked me to pick you up," he said, still smiling.

"Everyone today is called Ben," I said, laughing. "He is Ben, too, and I just left my brother, Ben, in Chicago."

We laughed together, then decided that I would ride with Ben, the student, since he could give me a taste of the college experience. I thanked Professor Ben for his kindness, and he promised to pick me up later in the week to show me his home and introduce me to his family.

I grabbed my bag, and we walked to the car. My feet were still cold because I didn't have the proper shoes for the snow, but I had my winter coat and leather gloves on. As I settled into Ben's car, one question crossed my mind: "Why do people live in Wisconsin when it's so cold?"

Ben knew about Cameroon because of our soccer team, which I was happy to boast about. Then, he told me about the International Programs Office's "Pick-Up Program," and I thought it was great that they helped pick up students like this. I asked him how I could help, and he said that once I got my driver's license, I could also help pick up other new students.

As we drove, I looked around and noticed that there were far more trees than I had expected to see in America. I didn't tell Ben what I was thinking, but I was very surprised. After about 35 minutes of driving, I saw lights as the city came into view ahead. We passed a few buildings that still seemed open at that time of the evening. It looked much later than it was.

Ben pulled up in front of Pray Sims Hall, which would be my home for the school year. He helped carry my duffel bag to the front desk. We greeted the desk attendants, who I later learned were also students. Everything felt so different from where I was coming from. Ben gave them my name, and after a few clicks on the computer, they handed me a package that contained my room key and some papers to read at my convenience.

Just before we left the front desk, I heard a soft voice call my name.

"Dinga." I looked around and saw a soft-spoken, gray-haired Asian gentleman who introduced himself as Dr. Fang.

We shook hands, and he thanked Ben for picking me up. He assured Ben that he would help me settle in.

We took the elevator up to the fourth floor, then walked through a hallway to my room. When we entered, I saw two beds. Dr. Fang explained that I would be sharing the room with another student, who would arrive in a few days.

He helped me unpack and even made my bed with me. This completely messed with my brain since back home, a man of his status helping me make my bed and showing me how things worked was just something I wasn't used to. In my country, someone of this stature wouldn't even need to know whether I had arrived or not. To top it all off, he asked if I was hungry and mentioned that there was a restaurant still open at that hour.

CHAPTER 10

The First Supper

"One who eats alone cannot discuss the taste of the food with others."
—*African proverb*

My brother had already talked about Dr. Fang, and I was curious to learn more about him. I was really happy to have finally met him. He took me to Perkins Restaurant, just a few minutes away from campus. We were seated in a booth by the window. I stared at the menu, and, having no idea what to order, I just followed his lead. I did not recognize most of the food on the menu. There seemed to be too many choices.

A waitress came up to us, smiling like she had known us for several months. She spoke very fast but kept smiling. Dr. Fang did most of the talking, as expected. He asked me what I would like to drink and listed a few things. He mentioned cranberry juice, and I recognized it from reading James Hadley Chase novels, so I ordered a glass with a smile, like a character in the novels. The waitress disappeared as fast as she had appeared.

Dr. Fang asked me how my flight was, and as I shared the little things that happened, the smiling waitress reappeared. This time, she brought a glass of water and a glass of cranberry juice. I tasted it and liked it very much. I thanked her for the drink, and she said, "No problem." I thought that was a strange way to respond. I couldn't remember anyone saying "No problem" after you said thank you, but since she was smiling, I believed her when she said there was no problem whatsoever. She asked if we were ready to order. Dr. Fang again did the talking and ordered pancakes for himself, which I thought was odd for dinner. He asked me if I wanted to try the baked potato and steak. That was the first time I heard of baked potatoes, although I had had potato and steak before, so I said sure.

The food arrived faster than I anticipated. Back home, time was always the last thing on anyone's mind when ordering food; no one rushed, and often they made dishes from scratch. The waitress delicately placed the plates in front of us, smiling all the while. Looking at my food, I noticed the potato still had its skin, but I hesitated to mention it. I wondered why, in a wealthy country like the United States, this restaurant couldn't afford a potato peeler. Perhaps, I reasoned, they left the skin on to keep the potato warm in the cold, snowy weather.

As if sensing my thoughts, Dr. Fang said, "You can eat it with the skin or just open it and eat the potato inside." I was relieved to have another option. We ate and talked more.

He told me he was both a part-time director of international programs and a psychology professor. I sat up straight, consciously following all the table manners my mother had taught me: closing my mouth while chewing, never talking with food in my mouth, and participating in conversation to avoid awkward silences. I was hyper-attentive to these details, determined not to make any mistakes during my first meal in America, especially in front of a director who happened to be a psychologist. I took smaller bites and stayed ready to respond or share something without risking food falling from my mouth. I believe I conducted myself well and enjoyed my meal, even though I avoided the potato skin. Throughout this time, I didn't worry about the bill, assuming, as in my culture, that when you invite someone to eat, you pay for their meal. This assumption would later come back to haunt me.

Dr. Fang paid for my meal and encouraged me to take the leftovers to my room. This custom was unfamiliar to me. He called it a "doggie bag," which piqued my curiosity. As a young man, I wondered what kind of special container this might be. Though the actual takeout container proved less exciting than I'd imagined, I was grateful to be able to bring my leftover food back to the dorm.

By the time Dr. Fang dropped me off, I was exhausted and ready for bed. I thanked him and said good night. I stood waiting for him to drive off before heading inside, while he remained in his car, watching and waving. I waved back. After this continued for a moment, he rolled down his window and asked if there was a problem. When I explained I was waiting for him to leave, he replied that he was waiting to make sure I got into the building safely. I chuckled at this final cultural misunderstanding of the evening, then turned and walked up the steps into the building.

In my room, I changed into the pajamas my brother had bought for me. As I climbed into bed, it felt as though I'd been traveling for a week. I tried to recall everything that had happened in the 48 hours since leaving my family, but sleep overcame me before I could finish the thought.

CHAPTER 11

Student Life

"Don't buy salt if you haven't licked it yet."
—*Ethiopian proverb*

As international students, we arrived on campus a few days before the rest of the student body to complete extensive orientation with the Foreign Student Office (FSO) staff. During orientation, all international students lived together in one hall, to be separated later when other students arrived. For our first meeting, we were instructed to gather in the building's basement at 2 p.m. Upon arrival, we selected our nametags and found seats, some choosing chairs while some of us sat on the carpeted floor.

I settled on the floor next to a gentleman, maybe in his late forties, with a well-trimmed gray beard. He wore a burgundy turtleneck sweater with slim-fitted blue jeans. He smiled and asked in a perfect American accent, "What's your name and where are you from?" Though I sensed he was neither foreign nor a student, I introduced myself as Samuel from Cameroon. "West Africa, correct?" he asked. "Yes," I replied, pleased that he knew my country's location. When he asked my age, I answered, but I wondered about the relevance of the question, as it is not customary in Africa to ask about one's age. Before I could ponder this further, Dr. Fang, the FSO director, announced, "We are pleased to have with us the chancellor of UWSP, Chancellor Tom George, and I'd like to invite him to say a few words of welcome." The man sitting beside me turned and said, "It was nice to meet you, Samuel, and good luck with school," then stood and walked toward Dr. Fang.

"I am Chancellor George, and I am very happy to..." he began, but I barely heard his words, lost in shock at what had just transpired. In Cameroon, I never saw a university chancellor without his extensive entourage, including security personnel. The highest administrator I had ever dared approach was the dean of the Law faculty—a meeting that took two weeks to arrange. Yet here at UWSP, I had been sitting casually on the floor with the chancellor of a university whose budget exceeded that of most Cameroonian cities.

When I later shared this experience with my brother, Ben, he advised me to expect more such encounters, explaining that most American leaders maintain a simple demeanor and don't surround themselves with security details and entourages. Indeed, I would later witness my classmates addressing professors by their first names rather than their titles.

My first day of class, a history course, was another memorable experience. I arrived twenty minutes early and chose a seat in the middle of the classroom. About five minutes before class, two students walked in, glanced at me, and stepped back out as if they'd entered the wrong room. Another student appeared, looked at me, then turned to the girls by the door and asked if this was the history classroom. Though I could hear them speaking, their words were unclear. Finally, the male student entered, followed by the two girls, and more students began filing in, taking seats throughout the room. Once everyone seemed settled, Professor Dr. Kent walked in and surveyed the class. Her eyes narrowed as if she wanted us to notice something, though she remained silent. Looking around, I realized all four chairs surrounding me were empty. I never asked Dr. Kent, but I suspect this was what caught her attention. She greeted us, introduced herself, and shared some personal background—I liked her immediately. After writing several dates on the board, she asked if anyone knew the corresponding historical events. The class fell silent. I looked around, wondering why no one wanted to speak up. After waiting a moment, I slowly raised my hand.

"Samuel, or do you go by Sam?" she asked.

"Sam is fine," I replied, then identified the historical events that matched each date. I correctly named all ten or so of them. She gave me an intrigued, somewhat puzzled look and said, "That was correct."

As I was leaving after class, Dr. Kent called me back. When I approached, she smiled and said, "That was impressive at the start of class." She inquired about my background, and I explained that I was from Cameroon, where we studied European history in middle school. Impressed, she thanked me for participating and encouraged me to continue contributing during her lessons. I left class that morning feeling elated.

The next day, more students filled the seats next to me, some smiling and even greeting me. One of the girls introduced herself, and we chatted for a bit before class. I enjoyed that class and did well in it. However, I struggled significant-ly with math.

Math has never been my strong suit, and in Cameroon, after middle school, students who choose the Arts track are not required to take math. As a result, I had been out of prac-tice for a long time before coming to UWSP. Even Math 90, the lowest level of college math, was a huge challenge for me. I hated the class and felt like the teacher was picking on me. When we worked on math problems involving money, I was completely lost because I barely understood the new cur-rency. Eventually, I stopped attending math class altogether. Somehow, I didn't realize that I had the option to drop the class, so I ended up with an "F."

Academically, it was a rough semester due to my struggles with math. I found it difficult to understand the writing style required in my courses, disliked the multiple-choice exams, and struggled to keep up with some professors who spoke too fast for me to comprehend. To be honest, I was unaware of the support services available on campus for struggling stu-dents. I don't recall anyone advising me on how to improve my situation.

I remember going to my room, shutting the door, and crying my eyes out. I didn't want to tell my brother, my par-ents, or anyone else. That evening, my phone rang—it was Ben. He told me that Dr. Fang had informed him that my grade point average had dropped and that I was at risk of losing my $2,000 scholarship. I was devastated and angry at everything and everyone.

Ben sent me a Greyhound ticket to visit them in Spring-field, Illinois. I desperately needed that break, so I was happy to go. The drive was long, but it gave me plenty of time to reflect on what I was doing and what I needed to change.

During the break, I had a wonderful time with my brother's wife and kids. My twin sister and I talked a lot and spent valuable time together. My brother kept encouraging me to work harder in school and to seek help from tutors when needed. At one point, he mentioned dropping a class instead of staying in it and failing. That caught my attention, so I asked him more about it and other aspects of the American education system. I learned so much from him during that break that I returned to school more determined to succeed.

The second semester flew by, and I became more involved on campus. I met regularly with Dr. Fang, who became my mentor and guided me toward campus resources.

Paying out-of-state tuition was not easy, and to make matters worse, one of my dad's banks went out of business, leaving him unable to support me financially. To cope, I took on additional on-campus jobs and skipped weekends and breaks so I could work as much as the law allowed. International students are limited to a maximum of 20 hours of on-campus work every two weeks and are not permitted to work off-campus unless they undergo a lengthy and expensive process to obtain a work permit. Eventually, I secured one because my father could no longer support me financially.

My schedule became increasingly busy and stressful. One day, after an especially exhausting day, I went online to check my email. As I logged into my account, I was thrilled to see a message from my girlfriend, Zoless, in Cameroon. Excited, I quickly opened the email. However, my excitement quickly turned to shock and then to anger. In the message, she told me that she had met someone else and wanted to spend the rest of her life with him. I read the email multiple times before responding simply: "I wish you all the best."

The following weeks were tough, but I knew I had to pull myself together and move forward. I channeled all my emotions into my schoolwork and jobs, and I became deeply involved on campus. Surprisingly, it turned out to be one of my best semesters, and I never looked back.

Since I was paying out-of-state tuition, I was determined to graduate as quickly as possible. I met with my academic advisor and mapped out a plan to complete my Sociology degree without a minor. By taking more credits than typically allowed and transferring some credits, I was able to complete the four-year program in just two years.

Graduation day was an unforgettable experience. My mother flew in from Cameroon to celebrate with my brother, friends, and other family members. I was overjoyed to be graduating. Though I was saddened that my father couldn't be there to see me walk across the stage, I was grateful for the presence of my loved ones who came to support me.

CHAPTER 12

She Kissed Her

"No medicine exists that can cure hatred."
—*African proverb*

At the university, I met students from many parts of the world. I made friends with students from South Korea, Saudi Arabia, Japan, Malaysia, Kenya, Singapore, the Ivory Coast, Nigeria, Ghana, and even the tiny country of Micronesia. As international students, we spent a lot of time together because we struggled to understand each other and because we all thought American food was too bland. I was particularly close to the students from Africa. Emmanuel, though born in the United States to Nigerian parents, was sent back to Nigeria, where he grew up, before later moving back to the United States. Yul was from the Ivory Coast. I learned that he did not speak a word of English when he arrived in the United States, but by the time I met him two years later, he was fluent. It was impressive to see what the English as a Second Language Program at the University of Wisconsin-Stevens Point (UWSP) could do. Geoffrey was from Kenya. He was very worldly, perhaps because he had lived and studied in South Africa before coming to the US. I found these three guys to be very smart and ambitious. I felt inspired when we hung out and talked about our different countries and Africa as a whole. Mohamed from Mali later became my roommate when I moved out of the dorms and rented off campus, and Wilfred from the Ivory Coast later joined us at UWSP.

We studied and worked hard during the week and enjoyed partying on weekends. We always started Friday nights at house parties and later went downtown to a local bar, *Brussar's,* that was the place to be. Everyone gathered at Brussar's for beer and music. There were usually many students and some non-students, generally from out of town. My friend Yul was a real party animal who always knew where the parties were and had a plan for how the night would unfold. Having a car gave Yul control over when things happened. I always looked forward to Friday nights because of the house parties and Brussar's. One of those nights, after hopping between a few house parties, typically in student houses with basements, we headed downtown to Brussar's. We were just a handful of black men in a sea of white students. There were times we joked that we were the endangered species to the white women. It always felt like the girls were watching us, trying to get our attention, or wanting to dance with us. Often, these dances ended with a make-out session on the dance floor. On this particular night, as the four of us streamed into the crowded bar, the latest song, "Hot in Herre" by the popular rapper Nelly, started playing. Yul and I slowly walked straight to the dance floor, moving with the rhythm of the song, where two young, beautiful white girls were dancing. They were holding each other close and dancing seductively to the song. We tried to smooth our way between them, but they held their position tight. We tried again, but they wouldn't relent their grip on each other.

At this point, we backed off and were quickly invited by a nearby willing group of three girls dancing a few feet from us. My eyes did not leave the pair who had rejected us. Now, it was not just that they were beautiful, but that they were unusually close to each other. Without any warning, they started kissing each other so gently that at first, I thought they were pretending. Then, on closer observation, I realized they were making out. This was so shocking to me that I left my dance partners, walked over to the two girls kissing, and asked them what had just happened.

They looked baffled by my question and asked me to repeat what I said. Instead of repeating my question, I asked them directly if they had just kissed each other. They started laughing at me. They continued laughing as they danced, still clutching each other. I still could not comprehend what I had observed. I asked them if they could do it again, just for me to be sure about what I thought I saw. Without hesitation, they started kissing again, ever so gently and passionately. I felt a hand on my shoulder, and I turned around to see my friend Yul laughing hard. He pulled me away from the two girls and ushered me toward the rest of our friends who had formed a gathering spot next to the bar. They must have observed me because they were all laughing. I wandered back awkwardly, still confused about the two girls kissing and why everyone was laughing. That was my first exposure to the LGBTQ+ world.

Later that year, I took a Women's Studies class to fill my schedule for the semester. On the first day of class, the professor asked each student why they had chosen to take the class. Most students gave thoughtful reasons for their enrollment. When she got to me, one of only two male students in the class, I said, jokingly, that I wanted to meet girls. The class erupted in laughter, but the professor did not find it funny. She moved on before I could formulate a proper response.

After a few weeks in that class, the professor invited students to an LGBTQ+ march happening downtown in Stevens Point. She asked for a show of hands from those who would attend the event. Everyone in class but me had their hands up as they looked around. The professor, who was beaming from the massive response, quickly changed her expression when she realized that I did not have my hand up. She came closer to me and asked politely but firmly why I would not be marching. I told her respectfully that I did not know enough to be out marching for or against anything. This time, she was not happy with me at all. She told me how this was very important to American women and to the LGBTQ+ community. I think this incident affected my relationship with the said professor and my subsequent final grade in that class. Ironically, my job responsibilities now include the retention, well-being, and graduation of all LGBTQ+ students at UWSP, and I served as Director of Diversity, Equity, and Inclusion at the Stevens Point Area Public School District. I have come a long way in learning about the LGBTQ+ community and the challenges they face throughout the world.

CHAPTER 13

Hospital Visit

"However long the night, the dawn will break."
—*African proverb*

One of the highlights of my time at UWSP was being part of the International Club, one of approximately 150 student organizations on campus. Commonly known as "I-Club," it was composed of students from various countries studying at the university. Most of the students were from China or other parts of Asia, likely influenced by the director of international programs, who was originally from Asia and had connections for recruiting students from the region.

Given the large number of Asian students, most of the I-Club's leaders were Asian as well. This was probably because it was easier for them to secure votes from fellow Asian students. It wasn't surprising, then, that when I decided to run for president of the I-Club, some of my African friends laughed at me to my face. They told me I was wasting my time and that any Asian student running against me would win by a landslide. However, undeterred by their remarks, I gathered the required signatures and filed the necessary paperwork.

During campaign week, I approached the process as if I were running for President of the United States. I formed a campaign team consisting of a campaign manager and a communications specialist to help design flyers. I also recruited a few Asian students to help me spread my platform among fellow Asian students.

I made four clear promises that I intended to fight for if elected president of the organization:

- First and foremost, I aimed to address the issue of our organization lacking office space on campus, despite being one of the largest student organizations.
- Secondly, I pledged to furnish the office without spending any of the organization's funds.
- Third, I promised to introduce a new winter activity to combat the winter blues.
- Lastly, I pledged to improve our elections by transitioning them online.

On the day of the campaign, the first candidate appealed to fellow Asian students, asking for their votes because she was from China and best understood their issues. The second candidate reminded the group that he had been actively involved with the club for the past two years and was, therefore, the best candidate.

When I took the stage, I quickly introduced my campaign team, thanked the outgoing officers, and then shared my four campaign goals. I went further by explaining how I planned to achieve them with a clear timeline. The group responded with huge applause, and at that moment, I knew I had done a great job.

The election lasted three days to ensure that everyone who wanted to vote had the opportunity. The results were announced via email. A friend informed me that they had been published, and I hurriedly checked my inbox. Scanning my emails, I spotted the one from the organization's web address. My name stood prominently at the top of the ticket as president. I had made history as the first non-Asian student to win the presidency in at least 10 years, based on available records. Congratulations poured in from I-Club members, club advisers, and my friends. I called my brother, Ben, to share the great news, and he was very proud of my achievement.

I immediately got to work fulfilling my campaign promises. I secured an office space, and by the end of the week, it was furnished with used items from different departments. I organized our leadership team to maintain office hours, keeping the office open at all times. Additionally, I met with my team and proposed a "Winter Olympics" to be held mostly indoors. We agreed and organized the first I-Olympics, featuring soccer, basketball, and volleyball tournaments. I dedicated the roving trophy to Dr. Fang, the club's veteran advisor.

The one promise that proved difficult to fulfill was the implementation of electronic voting. This was not due to a lack of effort but because the university did not have the necessary software to differentiate I-Club members from the rest of the student body at the time.

During the I-Club Winter Olympic Games, I played on a soccer team, and we dominated the tournament. I was having a great time until I collided with an opposing player. Immediately, I knew something was wrong because my left ankle felt detached from the rest of my body. The pain was intense, and I asked my friend Ellis Miles, who had a car, if he could take me to the hospital next to campus. He quickly brought his car around, and we headed to the hospital. On the way, he advised me to go to urgent care rather than the emergency room, explaining that it would be much cheaper. This was my first time visiting an American hospital.

The facility was spacious, spotlessly clean, and lacked the strong hospital smell I was accustomed to in Cameroon. Every hospital in Cameroon carries a distinct odor—a mixture of medicine, sweat, and what I always imagined death would smell like. It's a terrible, overpowering scent that can be recognized from miles away.

At the front desk, a woman asked me general questions, such as my name, age, address, and the reason for my visit. Most importantly, she wanted to know if I had insurance and asked to see my insurance card. I knew I had paid for insurance, but I had no idea how it worked. Ellis stepped in and explained that I was an international student with a different insurance plan. They talked for several minutes before the woman suggested that I go to the emergency room instead. She explained that my insurance would cover an emergency room visit without requiring a referral, whereas urgent care might not be fully covered.

None of this made any sense to me. In Cameroon, when you're sick, you simply go to the hospital and see a doctor or nurse. This complicated talk of insurance, costs, and the distinction between urgent care and the emergency room was completely new and overwhelming, especially while I was in so much pain.

Frustrated, Ellis told me to get back in the car. As we drove back to campus, he was visibly angry, cursing under his breath and speeding away from the hospital. We arrived on campus and called the director of the Foreign Student Office, Dr. Fang, who promptly showed up at our dorm. He listened to Ellis and asked us to follow his car back to the hospital. He went to the desk and spoke to the ladies there. They spoke for about thirty minutes before I was ushered to a waiting room, where a nurse came in and was very pleasant. Everyone who attended to me was so nice that I started to worry if they thought I was going to die.

The doctor came in and introduced himself, as the nurses had done. He sat down next to me, examined my ankle thoroughly, and ordered an X-ray for my foot. The X-ray team was equally friendly and very nice. To be honest, I had never experienced that level of customer service before. I wondered whether it was because Dr. Fang came to talk to them, or if this is what it means to be a patient in an American hospital. I had just experienced first-world healthcare for the first time, and I was impressed with the service I received despite the insurance debacle. I returned to the consulting room and met with the doctor, who reviewed my X-ray reports and concluded there were no broken bones. He said it was a hard sprain and a strain on the muscles and tendons. He prescribed some medications, which we picked up at the nearest pharmacy.

Several weeks passed, and I received a letter in the mail. It was a bill asking me to pay for the services because my insurance company had declined to pay the balance. After all, I was playing a "club sport." There was a number to call if I had any questions. I sure had some questions, so I called the number, and the lady on the other end mainly explained what was in the letter. I tried to explain to her that the club sport was the I-club and not like Manchester United Club or something. She encouraged me to call the insurance company and explain what I just told her. I called the insurance information on the back of my card.

Now, this second call was completely different from the first. The representative was far less pleasant; I suspect she was having a bad day. She insisted the insurance company wouldn't cover club sports. I explained that the term "club" didn't mean I played for the university or a professional soccer team. She countered that their records showed I participated in club sports. I clarified that yes, I had said that because that's what we call our student organizations: "clubs." She requested proof that I wasn't playing organized team sports, so I asked the athletic director to write me a letter. After mailing it, I waited two weeks, during which I received another notice from the hospital requesting payment. A few days after the second notice, a third letter arrived stating the insurance company had agreed to pay part of my bill, leaving me with about $200.

I called the number on the bill and spoke with another representative. I asked why I still owed $200 despite having insurance. She explained that I had to meet my insurance deductible, which was a completely new concept to me. I admitted that I didn't understand most of what she had explained. Though I could tell she was growing weary of explaining these concepts to someone with a thick accent, I thanked her and began researching insurance terms like copays and deductibles. The more I read and discussed with others, the more complicated it became. Paying the $200 from my $245 paycheck made for a difficult two weeks until my next payday.

A few weeks later, I received another bill, this time from a radiologist in nearby Wausau. I called the billing office again and reached a different representative. I questioned who this radiologist was, arguing that I hadn't visited Wausau and didn't remember any radiologist examining my X-rays during my consultation. She calmly explained that doctors routinely send X-rays to radiologists for second opinions. This seemed excessive to me, especially since the doctor had been certain it was just a sprain with no broken bones. I told her that since I hadn't agreed to any second opinion, I wouldn't pay this bill.

Several weeks later, I received another bill, now increased by late payment penalties. I called again to reaffirm that I wouldn't pay. Several months passed without any communication from the billing office. I thought I had succeeded by clearly and firmly refusing to pay the bill.

A few months later, when I was ready to purchase my first car in America, I learned another important lesson about unpaid bills. The car was a 1999 white Chrysler Sebring. I spoke to the bank and was approved for a $5,000 loan. I was thrilled until I received a call from the bank informing me that they couldn't process the loan because my bill had been sent to collections.

Confused, I asked why, by whom, and what exactly "collections" meant. The bank representative gave me a phone number to call for more information. I promptly called and was told that they had my bill and that I had 24 hours to clear the total balance, or it would become a police matter. I panicked. I asked the collection agency how the process worked and why my bill had been sent to them, but they refused to explain. Instead, they called me almost every hour, reminding me that time was running out.

I explained my situation, telling them my check would take about three days to reach them. They insisted I use a debit or credit card instead. Worried, I went to my bank and explained what was happening. The bank manager assured me that there would be no police involvement and encouraged me to write a check and mail it, which I did.

Despite informing the collection agency that my check was on the way, the calls continued for the next three days, escalating with various threats. One person even called me the "scum of the earth" and said I deserved death. I was terrified. Then, suddenly, the calls stopped.

A few days later, I called the bank to confirm the check had cleared. They informed me that the payment had gone through, but the collection had left a stain on my credit score. The bank provided contact information for credit reporting agencies, but reaching someone was frustratingly difficult. When I finally spoke to a representative, I was told there was nothing they could do. They advised me to pay my future bills on time and assured me that my credit history would improve over time.

When I called the bank again, I was met with more bad news; they were no longer willing to approve my loan unless I had a cosigner. Another new term I had to learn. I made several calls, and the only person who agreed to cosign for me was my "American father," Richard Okray. He came to the bank, signed as my cosigner, and helped me secure the $5,000 loan.

We went to the dealership with the bank's check and finalized the transaction. I was overjoyed, but throughout the process, I couldn't help but reflect on how my lack of knowledge of the healthcare system had almost cost me the chance to achieve the milestone of owning a car in America.

CHAPTER 14

Jump-starting my Battery

"The eye never forgets what the heart has seen."
—*African proverb*

On a beautiful, sunny day during my final semester at the University of Wisconsin–Stevens Point, I was studying in the computer lab when someone slowly sat down in the seat next to me. I glanced over and immediately recognized the face.

"Hey, I think I know you," I said.

"Yes, you and your friends came to our apartment," she said, smiling.

I smiled back, remembering that visit. A couple of my friends knew her and her roommate, so we had stopped by their place a few weeks prior. During that visit, I had been somewhat aloof, and she had told me I was "standoffish." In reality, I had kept my distance because my friends had been busy flirting with the two girls and trying to get their phone numbers. Since they lived out of town and I didn't expect to see them again, I didn't want to "waste" my charm.

Seeing her again in the computer lab was a pleasant surprise. I asked for her name once more, and she replied, "Amy." We chatted for a bit, and I mentioned that my car wouldn't start that morning and I had no idea what was wrong. She asked if there had been a clicking sound when I turned the key. I admitted I hadn't noticed and didn't even understand what that meant. She explained that a clicking sound usually indicated a battery issue and that my car probably just needed a jump-start. I was amazed because I had never heard that before, let alone from a girl talking about cars like that.

Then she asked if I had jumper cables. I sheepishly admitted I didn't even know what those were. She gave me a look that seemed to say, *Are you serious?* Then, as if deciding I wasn't completely hopeless, she smiled in a way that said, *That's cute.* I much preferred that look.

She offered to come by my apartment after school and help me jump-start my car since she had jumper cables. After class, we met where she packed her black 2001 Saturn, and we drove for five minutes to my apartment. She parked next to my 1999 Chrysler Sebring and told me to "pop the hood."

That was another phrase I had never heard before. I must have given her a confused look because she repeated it twice before I finally admitted I had no idea what she meant. At that moment, I felt like I was losing all my points. She got out of her car, opened my door, reached under the steering wheel and pressed something. I heard a click. Then, walking to the front of the car, she slipped her fingers under the hood, caressed something unseen, and—voilà—popped the hood.

"This is how you pop the hood," she announced.

I stood there, speechless, watching her as she pulled out a small black bag from her car. From inside, she retrieved a set of jumper cables, black and red cords with crab-like clamps. She expertly connected her car to mine, moving between them with a confidence that left me in awe. I had no idea what she was doing, but she did. Then she told me to get in and start my car. Like magic, the engine roared to life. She had not only jump-started my car—she had jump-started my heart.

"Let it run for a while!" she shouted over the noise of the two engines.

I stood there, watching our cars connect, looking at her in complete amazement. At that moment, I felt something I hadn't felt in a long time.

Amy and I spent more time together after that. She told me she had one class in Stevens Point but had to drive 45 minutes to Wausau for another, only to return early in the morning for a class. Wanting to make things easier for her, I offered my apartment as a place to stay on those nights. She accepted, and as time passed, we grew closer.

After a while, I asked her to be my girlfriend. She hesitated at first, as I was still transitioning out of another relationship. Eventually, we started dating. Amy attended my graduation and met some of my family members. My mother liked her instantly, and at that moment, I knew she was the one. Later, when my father visited the United States, he also met Amy and her family, and he liked them just as much. I was very nervous about my dad meeting Amy because I had not informed him that she was Caucasian. I worried about what he would say, but he focused on the person and not her skin color. As for the broader society, I am personally grateful for the sacrifices of biracial couples who came before me.

The journey toward acceptance of biracial marriage in America has been long and fraught with struggles, shaped by both legal battles and tragic historical events. One of the most significant milestones in this fight was the 1967 Supreme Court case *Loving v. Virginia*, which struck down laws banning interracial marriage. This landmark decision laid the foundation for a society in which love, rather than race, determines the legitimacy of a union.

Before *Loving v. Virginia*, interracial relationships were met with hostility, and in many states, they were outright illegal. The brutal killing of Emmett Till in 1955 serves as a painful reminder of the dangers Black men faced simply for being perceived as showing interest in White women. Till, a 14-year-old Black boy from Chicago, was lynched in Mississippi after being falsely accused of flirting with a white woman. His death exposed the deep-seated racism in America and became a catalyst for the Civil Rights Movement.

Just over a decade later, the *Loving* case challenged these racist structures head-on. Richard and Mildred Loving, a White man and a Black woman, were arrested in Virginia for being married. Their case reached the Supreme Court, which unanimously ruled that laws prohibiting interracial marriage were unconstitutional. This decision not only affirmed the right to love freely but also set the stage for future generations to embrace diversity in relationships.

Today, thanks to the struggles of those who loved before me and fought for equality in marriage, a Black immigrant from Cameroon can marry a White woman from Medford, Wisconsin, without fear of legal repercussions or societal rejection on the scale seen in the past. While challenges and prejudices still exist, the progress made since Emmett Till's time and the *Loving* decision has created a society where interracial couples can build lives together without the legal and violent obstacles of the past. The fight for equality in love continues, but the legacy of those who fought for it ensures that love, in all its forms, remains protected and celebrated.

In 2005, I proposed to Amy, and we got married in 2006. Our wedding was a blend of typical Midwestern traditions sprinkled with my African customs and practices. I can venture to say that Medford, WI, saw more black people in its history. Given that this was my first experience at a Midwest wedding, there were a few things that were very new to my family and I. The grand match, the "hokky poky" dance and the YMCA song played a few times more than I cared for. What really threw me off was that almost half the hall emptied out after dinner, and I thought the event was winding down early. After about an hour and a half, they all returned, and I later learned that the farmers went to feed and milk the cows. Then the dance really kicked into high gear. Most of my family members and friends drank Heineken and found the wedding an interesting experience as it was their first, too.

Our first son, Sivan, was born in 2007. As of this book's publication in 2025, Sivan is a senior at our local high school. He serves as the captain of the soccer team and finished the season with a great record. His passion for soccer is evident, and his leadership on the field is inspiring. In addition to soccer, he plays varsity basketball as a point guard, demonstrating his versatility as an athlete. Attending his games has become a family tradition, and we take great pride in cheering him on.

Sivan has always been highly competitive. Even as a child, he was determined to keep track of the score and insisted that games continue until he had a fair chance at winning. While his passion for competition drives him to excel, losses can be tough for him to handle. I always hope that through conversations and guidance from his coaches, he will continue to develop a balanced perspective on both winning and losing.

Now that Sivan is driving, managing schedules has become much easier, as we no longer have to coordinate all his pick-ups and drop-offs. He also helps his younger brother, Sander, occasionally after practices and games, showing his growing sense of responsibility both on and off the field. Sivan would like to study Business, Communications and Marketing in college.

Sander was born in 2009 and was always a content, self-soothing baby. Like his older brother, he has a deep love for sports. He played football in junior high before shifting his focus to basketball and now plays on his high school's JV team.

Beyond athletics, Sander's independence shines through in many ways. He showed early interest in cooking and learned from my wife and I and his uncle Noah, who briefly lived with us to complete college. He enjoys experimenting with new recipes. He is also a thoughtful and engaging conversationalist, eager to discuss a wide range of topics, from politics and social justice to cooking, cars, and family dynamics. His passion for advocacy is evident in his leadership role as president of the student club, *Junior Advocates for Change and Equity*. With a strong sense of purpose and ambition, he is already exploring college options as he looks ahead to his future beyond high school.

Sage was born in 2012 and was immediately adored by his two older brothers, who were eager to teach him everything they knew until they realized they often had to slow down to match his age and abilities, which occasionally frustrated them. From an early age, Sage displayed an inquisitive nature, asking adults thought-provoking questions far beyond his years, often catching them off guard.

He explored both volleyball and basketball in elementary school and his first year of junior high, but ultimately decided they weren't for him. As he put it, *"I didn't like the return on my investment."* He felt that the competitive nature of the games took away the fun.

Sage's interests evolve over time, and he enjoys different subjects at different stages of his education. His career aspirations have also shifted, but for a long time, he was determined to become a *"hotshot lawyer."* When asked to define the term, he confidently explained that regular lawyers do the work, while hotshot lawyers do the talking and make a lot of money.

With a large circle of friends, Sage loves spending weekends hanging out, playing video games, and indulging in chips and sugary drinks. His sharp wit, curiosity, and social nature continue to shape his unique personality.

Our only daughter, Amiya, was born in 2014, making her entrance into the world in grand style. That unforgettable day began with my wife informing me that her water had broken—we needed to get to the hospital immediately. I had just bought a brand-new Toyota Camry Hybrid with fresh leather seats, but there was no time to think about that. We jumped in the car and sped toward the hospital in Weston, a 30-minute drive away, as I cruised down Highway 39 at 75 miles per hour, well above the speed limit. I kept my hazard lights on and stayed on the phone with the hospital, updating them as my wife twisted and turned in the passenger seat.

When we arrived at the hospital entrance, a medical team was already waiting. The lead nurse took one look at my wife and knew the baby was on her way, right there in the car. I rushed to help, but the staff quickly took over, moving with expert precision. In a frantic, chaotic scene, they delivered Amiya right there in the front seat. A few tense moments later, she let out a strong cry, and relief washed over us. Still attached to her umbilical cord, she was bundled up and taken inside with my wife to complete the birthing process. I, on the other hand, drove to the parking lot, already thinking about how to clean my once-pristine leather seats now infused with the unmistakable scent of newborn life.

For a brief moment, I naively thought that since Amiya was born in the parking lot, the hospital bill might be reduced. Unfortunately, that was not the case since we still had to pay the full amount. But none of that mattered; we were overwhelmed with joy at finally welcoming a daughter after three boys.

However, our excitement soon turned to concern when Amiya didn't pass meconium—the black stool that newborns typically release after birth. Doctors initially suspected a possible intestinal complication, but further tests and X-rays led them to consider cystic fibrosis (CF), a genetic disorder that affects the lungs and digestive system. Given my African heritage, the doctors were skeptical at first, but genetic testing quickly confirmed that my wife and I were both carriers of different CF variants. In a surprising twist, my own DNA analysis revealed something unexpected. I was 15% Irish, traced back three generations on my mother's side.

We named our daughter Amiya Lucia, giving her the initials *AL* after her mother, as we had agreed. Despite the challenges of living with CF, Amiya is a resilient and joyful child. She takes medications to help her digest food and undergoes vest therapy to clear mucus from her lungs. But beyond her treatments, Amiya is a light in our lives, full of kindness, energy, and creativity. She loves singing, dancing, and arts and crafts. She knows everyone in the neighborhood and makes friends effortlessly, always showing genuine care for others.

Amiya's entrance into the world was dramatic, but it was just the beginning of her incredible journey. She continues to amaze us every day with her strength, warmth, and unwavering spirit.

There is an eight-year gap between Amiya and our youngest child, Sable, who was born in 2022. Though no one wants to admit it outright, his arrival was a complete surprise. From the moment we learned that we were expecting another child, we were filled with both excitement and anxiety, particularly about the possibility of Sable inheriting cystic fibrosis (CF) or another genetic condition. To ease our concerns, we went the extra mile, testing the fetus for every potential health issue to ensure he was viable. Doctors warned us that if he had CF, it could make cohabiting with Amiya extremely challenging, adding even more stress as we anxiously awaited the test results.

On the other hand, we also discovered a potential silver lining—Sable's umbilical cord blood could one day aid in Amiya's treatment with the new CF therapies being developed. So, when he was born, Amy arranged for a company to store his cord blood for several years, hoping it might benefit Amiya in the future.

Sable is a joyful and energetic child, always eager to keep up with his older siblings. Like his brothers, he has taken a strong interest in soccer and basketball. But his bond with Amiya is something special—her name was the first he could say clearly. He can hardly wait for her to return from school each day, eagerly anticipating their love-hate play sessions. Amiya enjoys spending time with him, but when she wants to be with her friends without her little brother tagging along, Sable protests loudly, often in tears, before reluctantly settling for time with his parents.

Despite the unexpected nature of his arrival, Sable has brought immeasurable joy to our family, his presence strengthening the bonds between his siblings in ways we never could have predicted.

CHAPTER 15

Pain

"Happiness was but the occasional episode in a general drama
of pain."
—*Thomas Hardy*

My happiness was shattered in June of 2009. Remember my sister Ma Kah, who went with me to the U.S. embassy to get a visa? I had gotten word that she was sick. I called her, and we spoke for about an hour. We talked about her health, life in America, and our family. She told me that she was very sick with a stomach complication and was hoping to get surgery in a few days.

Three days later, as I pulled into the driveway at my workplace, my phone rang. It was my brother Jacob from Oklahoma. His voice was cracking, and he was almost whispering. "Ma Kah is dead." I felt numb. My heart sank, and my throat felt tight. I managed to put the car in park and stared straight through the windshield. As I sat in my car, I just could not fathom a world without my sister. I felt the tears streaming down my cheeks, and I did nothing to stop them.

I must have been in the car for about 20 minutes when my phone rang again. It was my work asking if I was coming to the 8:30 a.m. meeting. I wiped my eyes and went into the office to join the team. For the first 10 minutes of the meeting, I honestly did not hear anything anyone was saying. As soon as my supervisor asked me what I thought of what they were discussing, I just started crying again, taking everyone off guard. They all looked at each other, and my boss cleared the room and asked me what was going on. I did my best to compose myself and told him what had happened. He was very sorry about it and ordered me to take some time off. It was a very difficult week, and many difficult months after that day.

The emotion of losing someone is something that I don't think anyone can truly describe. The best way I can describe it is like a fern slowly taking over a piece of land, engulfing everything in sight. I struggled to stay strong or take charge of my life, but I was slowly drifting into a long daze each day. I spoke to my other family members as often as I could, but my pain was constant. I started realizing I wasn't fully present at meetings or events. I started getting worried about what was happening to me. I read books about loss, grief, and coping strategies. I read about depression but quickly dismissed it as a "White people thing." This thought occurred to me mostly because most, if not all, of my searches returned videos of White people talking about their experiences. Even the articles I read seemed to address White folks, as far as I understood. It wasn't until later that I realized that people of color suffer from depression too, when someone very dear to me in my family shared with me their struggles with depression and the treatment they were receiving. It is worth mentioning that depression remains a significant but often overlooked issue in African American communities, especially among immigrants. Historically, mental health struggles have been misunderstood, with depression sometimes being dismissed as a "Caucasian disease" rather than a legitimate concern within our communities. This misconception stems from cultural narratives that emphasize resilience, religious faith, and self-reliance, often discouraging open discussions about mental health. My family is no exception to this school of thought.

The implications of this mindset are profound. Many African Americans suffering from depression go undiagnosed or untreated, leading to worsening symptoms, strained relationships, poor work performance, and even increased suicide rates, particularly among men. The stigma surrounding mental health also prevents individuals from seeking therapy, as it is sometimes viewed as a sign of weakness or a betrayal of cultural strength. It is generally seen as something that brings shame to the individual and their family. Additionally, systemic barriers such as limited access to culturally competent healthcare providers further complicate the issue.

To address these challenges, education and awareness about mental health must be prioritized. Community leaders, religious institutions, and trusted figures should work to normalize discussions about depression and promote the benefits of seeking professional help. Increasing access to Black mental health professionals and culturally relevant therapy can also bridge the gap between stigma and treatment. I think I can count with one hand the number of mental health professionals from Cameroon, let alone from my ethnic group. This makes it difficult to find a trusted provider who understands the cultural context of what Africans are going through. Furthermore, incorporating holistic approaches, such as community support groups, spiritual guidance, and culturally sensitive counseling, can help reshape the narrative around mental health in African American communities.

Breaking the cycle of silence surrounding depression is crucial for the well-being of the Black community. By acknowledging and addressing mental health issues, African Americans can foster a healthier, more supportive environment for those in need.

CHAPTER 16

First Visit Back to Cameroon

"Only a fool will test the depth of the river with both feet."
—*African proverb*

When I first boarded the plane from Cameroon to the United States, I believed I was heading toward clarity, toward a place where I could finally define who I was meant to be. But what I found on the other side was not certainty, but fragmentation. I was no longer entirely Cameroonian, and not yet truly American. I lived in the spaces between languages, customs, and identities. In America, I was the outsider with an accent and a story no one quite knew how to receive. Heading back to Cameroon was a quest to find my rhythm to a familiar distance, but I was dreading the silent question in my head: *Have you changed too much to still belong here?*

I did not go home for my sister's burial because I was finishing my master's degree and still waiting to receive my green card to adjust my immigration status through marriage. But in June of 2010, my family was celebrating the lives of my sister and my grandmother, Anna Tangwi, who had passed away a couple of years before my sister. By this time, I had graduated in May and received my green card as a permanent resident of the United States, so I was eager to travel back to Cameroon for the celebrations.

The flight was long, filled with anticipation and mixed emotions. I was traveling with a family friend, Maximillian Okray. I met Max in 2002 when he was about eight years old. The University of Wisconsin-Stevens Point had a program called "The Host Family Program," which paired foreign students with families in the community. These families did not host the students in their homes; rather, the relationships were flexible, allowing students and their assigned families to interact as much or as little as they wished. I was paired with Richard (Dick) and Carol Okray and their three children: Hannah, Xerxis, and Max.

At the first host family meeting, Carol and the kids couldn't attend because they had just returned from a trip to Europe. Instead, Dick came, introduced by Carol's mother, who was on the committee that paired students with families. Dick was tall, incredibly handsome, with piercing eyes. He wore sweatpants, a sweatshirt, and leather sandals with socks—seemingly unfazed by the winter cold. He spoke with a constant smile in his eyes, and I liked him instantly.

He quickly apologized for Carol's absence due to jet lag, shared a little about their recent trip, and asked about my family. He fired off a series of questions about my home, my major, and my goals, listening intently. I hoped he could understand me despite my heavy accent.

Later, the students were asked to introduce their host families. When it was my turn, I told the group that my host family owned a potato farm and promised to take all the students to visit "our" farm someday. I made sure to keep that promise. Later that summer, I invited the students to visit the Okray Family Farms, where we enjoyed a wonderful meal of baked potatoes at their home.

I have a great and very close relationship with the Okray family. One of the Okray kids, Xerxis, stood up at our wedding. Max, however, became a close friend of mine as he grew older. One day, as we were having a BBQ party at my house with the Okrays in attendance, I started talking about my upcoming trip to Cameroon. Carol almost casually said, "Take Max with you." I looked over at Max, and his eyes lit up. As the days and weeks went by, the idea became more likely to come to fruition. Carol was very proactive in obtaining all the required documents to allow Max to travel with me. Max was just 17 years old at the time, so his parents had to sign a permit allowing me to take him out of the country.

When the day came to travel, Dick and Carol drove us to Chicago, where we would catch our flight to Cameroon. The traffic in Chicago was terrible, and Dick was very impatient. We inched our way toward the airport until the traffic eased up as we approached O'Hare. Dick pulled up at the curb and helped us unload our bags. We hugged, and they wished us luck. I don't know what Max was thinking at the time, but we were preoccupied with navigating the huge airport. The security process was tedious. We weighed our bags and shuffled things from one to another to make sure they all weighed 50 lbs (23 kg) or less. We both checked two bags each and had smaller carry-ons for the plane.

We went through security and sat down in the general lounge area, waiting for our boarding time, 45 minutes later. Max and I talked about what to expect. As I shared what

I knew with Max, I began to realize how much I might not know after being gone for nine years. I began feeling anxious about the trip. It dawned on me that I was going to a place that had always been home but now seemed unfamiliar in its details. I could talk more eloquently about Stevens Point than about Cameroon or Bali, my hometown. This thought recurred throughout most of the trip. I tried to use this time to ask Max about what he expected to get out of the trip. He appeared very excited to explore the country and meet new people.

The captain announced that we were descending into Douala, Cameroon. We were reminded to sit down, fasten our seat belts, and straighten our seats. As I performed these rituals, my heart began to beat faster. The huge Boeing 747 continued to slice through the blue and white skies toward Douala airport. My ears felt like balloons were being inflated in their inner chambers. About 20 minutes later, the plane emerged from the blue clouds as if by magic, and I could see the city of Douala clearly. My heart beat even faster. Swaying the huge plane in a graceful maneuver, the pilot seemed to be announcing to the people of Cameroon that their long-lost son was finally coming home. The plane hit the tarmac, and to my happy surprise, the passengers burst into applause for the pilot and crew. I joined the clapping and couldn't wait to ask why we were applauding. Everyone I asked had a different explanation, but the one I liked best was that landing at Douala airport is so tricky that when a pilot and crew succeed, passengers show their appreciation with loud applause. The plane taxied to the gate immediately since we were one of three planes on the runway. I was eager to get off the plane and see family members who were waiting to pick me up.

I stood up, collected my carry-on bag, and waited in line to disembark. About five to ten minutes went by before we could leave the plane. It took a while to get through security, immigration, and the Health Authorities, who checked our yellow fever cards to ensure our vaccines were up to date. The health service officers took their job so seriously that I began to wonder if there were more diseases in America than in Cameroon. Most people were from the three different planes that had arrived that evening. The room was hot, crowded, and disorganized. There were no lines, I thought, and the few police officers I saw seemed busy giving VIP treatment to passengers who could slip them a few CFA francs (Cameroon currency). The money changing hands was almost blatant. I was turned off by what I observed, but was too preoccupied with my excitement to see my family members on the other side of the immigration gate.

When it was our turn to get our passports stamped for entry at the immigration kiosk, the immigration officer motioned us to step forward. As we started walking, one of the "VIP" police officers stepped in front of us with four passports in his hand and a family of four on his heels. I was dumbfounded, but looking around, it seemed like that was business as usual. After about five minutes of reviewing their documents, the immigration officer stamped their passports and directed them to the baggage claim area. He then motioned Max and me forward again. For some strange reason, I expected an apology, but he looked at us as if nothing unusual had happened. We cleared immigration and continued to the baggage claim area.

In this section, the word chaos takes on a new meaning: Travelers were searching for their bags while porters in green vests, who appeared to be uniformed airport employees, practically forced themselves on travelers to carry their bags. Each porter had about five to ten baggage carts. I walked up to one and asked for a cart. He told me his price, and I quickly declined. He offered to help me get my things past customs. Only then, as he pointed to another barricade, did I notice I still had to go through another checkpoint. I brushed him and his baggage carts aside and moved closer to the conveyor belt, looking for the four bags that we had checked in at the Chicago airport.

It took a while, but we eventually found all four bags. We fought our way through the crowd of travelers, dodging baggage handlers who tried to "help" us and agents who offered to escort us through customs for a fee. We shuffled forward until we reached the customs barricade. An agent leaped forward and demanded to inspect our luggage. She opened three bags, roughly searching through them and leaving them open as she moved from one to another. She asked if we had anything we planned to sell, and we said no. After one final look in a bag, she waved us through. I scrambled to zip up the bags and moved forward to make way for others. I knew we didn't have anything of value that would warrant any "settlement" with customs, so I wasn't surprised when we were cleared to go.

As we exited the airport building to the curb, there was a complete blackout. The lights went out, and the whole place went dark. To tell you the truth, I was scared and deeply ashamed of my country. Here I was, coming back home after nine years with a friend I wanted to impress, and now this. Several people had flashlights, as if they had anticipated this happening. Among the flashlight beams, I heard a familiar voice call out—it was my cousin, Mado. She approached us with her flashlight. I was overjoyed to see her and gave her a huge embrace. She greeted Max with a hug, too and assured us the lights would soon come back on. As if on cue, they flickered back to life. That's when I realized most of the flashlights had come from cell phones. I was both amazed and impressed by this—I had left Cameroon when only the wealthy had cell phones, and now it seemed almost everyone carried a portable phone with a flashlight.

Other siblings came over to help with the bags, and we were ushered to a van in the parking lot. Max looked lost in the chaos but stayed quiet. I assured him that all was well and that my cousins would take care of us. The van was an 18-passenger vehicle in very poor condition. The driver secured our bags on top, and everyone got in. I sat between Max and Mado, trying to explain to Max about the bad roads, the garbage and the shacks along the roadside. Then I realized I was making excuses for things I felt embarrassed about. I had left Cameroon when these conditions seemed normal, but coming back from America, I felt ashamed of my home's dilapidated state. In a way, Cameroon seemed to have regressed during my nine years away. Everything felt very strange to me.

My father, Vincent, and my
mother, Magdalin.

My twin sister, Grace, and I
during a visit to Maryland,
USA.

My father, Senior
Superintendent of Police.

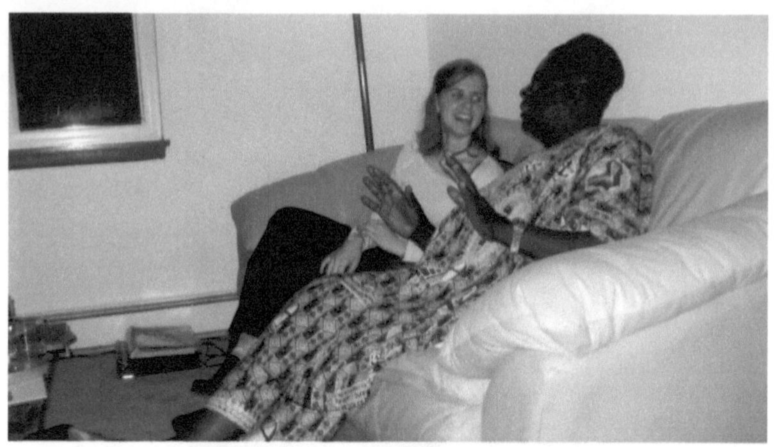

My father, Vincent, during his first meeting with my then-girl-
friend, Amy, who later became my wife.

My father, Vincent, and
I at the Douala Airport
in Cameroon on my first
departure, 2002.

Graduation day with my four best friends in college: Sam Dinga from Cameroon; Yul Ouattara from Ivory Coast; Geoffrey Mburu from Kenya; and Emmanuel Ukpong from Nigeria; 2004

My father, Vincent, adorns my son, Sivan Sigala, with a traditional hat during one of his visits to the United States.

The first time I
voted as a proud
American, with
my sons Sivan and
Sander.

Amy and I during
our wedding
in Medford,
Wisconsin, 2006.

My son, Sander, and
I taking a walk at a
lake in Wisconsin,
2009.

My sister, Cathrine Dinga, who finally became a lawyer as my father wished.

My sister, Ma Kah Rosemary Dinga, of blessed memory.

With most of my siblings at one of my niece's weddings in Chicago, IL, in 2022.

Growing up in Victoria (Limbe) with my siblings: Dr. Tina; Catherine, Esq.; Dr. Vera; Dr. Sam; and Peter (Ba Tita).

My mother, Magdalin, and her twin sister, Mary.

My wife and our five children: Sivan, Sander, Sage, Amiya, and Sable.

My father, Vincent, and my
mother, Magdalin, in Bali
Nyonga.

My father, Vincent, and my stepmother,
Cecilia, in Bali Nyonga.

My friend, Wilson, and I during summer holidays
in Bali Nyonga.

My father, Vincent,
and my wife, Amy,
in Bali Nyonga,
2012.

My father, Vincent, my mother, Magdalin, my wife, Amy, and myself at our first home in Bamenda, Cameroon.

Orphans at the Bon Makah Orphanage & Resource Center in Douala, Cameroon, 2025.

My brother, Ben, and I during my doctoral
graduation in Madison, Wisconsin, 2015.

CHAPTER 17

Cameroon

"Home is not where we live, it is a place we belong."
—*African proverb*

The concept of *Sankofa* originates from the Akan people of Ghana and is symbolized by a bird with its head turned backward, retrieving an egg from its back. The term *Sankofa* translates to "return and get it," emphasizing the importance of looking to the past to inform and guide the future. I often felt the need to return to Cameroon to better understand why I could fit in America but not feel like I truly belonged.

In the 1470s, the first Portuguese explorers landed on the coast of Cameroon via the Bight of Biafra, encountering a picturesque stream teeming with vibrant orange prawns or shrimp. Mistakenly, they dubbed the land the "River of Prawns" or "River of Shrimp."

Fast-forward to 1884, when Cameroon fell under German colonization, christened *Kamerun*, until their defeat in World War I in 1916 by the Allied powers. Post-war, the nation was bifurcated: the eastern sector, approximately 80%, was ceded to the French for administration alongside other colonized territories such as Chad, Congo, and Gabon. Meanwhile, the southern portion was administered by the British as part of their larger colony, Nigeria. The two colonial powers employed contrasting governance approaches: direct rule by the French, entailing cultural assimilation and French administrative oversight, versus indirect rule by the British, which maintained local authorities' autonomy under colonial oversight.

By 1960, African nations, including French Cameroon, had begun demanding independence from their colonial overlords. Following a contentious plebiscite in 1961, Southern Cameroons opted to unite with French Cameroon to achieve independence. This amalgamation resulted in a bilingual nation, in which 20% spoke English as their primary language, adhered to common law, and received an education under the Anglo-Saxon system, while the remaining 80% predominantly spoke French, practiced civil law, and adopted French cultural norms. While French Cameroon had a president, English Cameroon retained its prime minister and House of Representatives, embodying a semblance of semi-autonomy within the union.

This newfound independence ushered in socio-economic progress, akin to that of other African nations emerging from colonial rule. Cameroon became a peaceful nation, fervently passionate about soccer and music. Congolese tunes and local Cameroonian music, such as *Makossa*, captivated the populace, as major urban centers such as Douala, Yaoundé, Bamenda, and Buea flourished into bustling commercial and political hubs, characterized by cleanliness and vibrant energy akin to that of contemporary metropolises.

Because of my father's profession, we had the opportunity to explore and live in various cities across the country. Among them, Victoria (now Limbe) holds a special place in my heart. What captivated me most at a young age were the traffic police officers, impeccably attired in white gloves and boot covers, exuding stern professionalism as they skillfully managed traffic in the city center.

In Victoria, it was common to see women and children bustling about on designated days, hurriedly depositing trash for collection by passing garbage trucks. Mornings were punctuated by the melodic calls of the milkman, offering fresh milk to those in need, and the distinctive horn of the bread truck signaling its route through the neighborhood for eager patrons seeking freshly baked loaves. Life unfolded simply, with each element seemingly falling into its rightful place.

Fast forward several decades, and I find myself seated on a bus alongside my young friend, Max, struggling to explain the Cameroon I have returned to. As we journeyed through the dimly lit streets of Douala, I couldn't help but ponder the transformation that had befallen the country. The roads, once smooth and well-marked, now lay pockmarked with countless potholes, turning the journey into a bumpy, chaotic affair. Drivers navigated with reckless abandon, paying little heed to any semblance of road signage that may have once existed. The cacophony of car horns and the sight of motorbikes, often carrying multiple passengers, overwhelmed the bustling thoroughfares.

I recalled a time when motorbikes were a rare sight, primarily reserved for private use. However, a deal struck between the Cameroon and Chinese governments flooded the streets with affordable Chinese-made bikes, now ubiquitous as taxis. These two-wheeled vehicles, dubbed "harmful insects" by one of my cousins in the van, elicited laughter but also prompted contemplation of the consequences of this unregulated influx, facilitated by government agreements.

I began asking questions about the cost of a brand-new bike, the average rider's age, the training they received, and licensing or insurance requirements. Almost all riders and their passengers were helmetless, and only a few wore fluorescent jackets or vests to help other road users notice them. I continued to ask questions, wondering what I could do to help with the issues I could readily identify.

One of my cousins in the van interrupted my thoughts, commenting that the bikes had helped the poor by providing affordable rides and creating jobs for high school and university graduates who couldn't find work. This statement quickly made me realize how at odds I was with the people I was already formulating strategies to help. While I saw the bikes as road hazards, the government likely viewed them as a means to ease unemployment and promote economic empowerment for the younger population, which made up more than 70% of the total population.

After driving for about 45 minutes, we pulled into a dark driveway, and my cousin announced, "Here we are." Her apartment was humble yet welcoming. She offered us cold water, a much-needed relief from the scorching heat that hovered around 95°F. Max appeared to be sweating profusely, prompting concern of dehydration, so I insisted he shower first. Meanwhile, I sent someone to procure bottled water for us, recognizing the critical importance of clean water—a resource scarce for over a billion people worldwide.

Upon its arrival, the bottled water was lukewarm, but its purity brought solace. Our physicians in the United States had adamantly cautioned against consuming anything not sealed in a bottle, emphasizing the paramount importance of hygiene. For dinner, my cousin prepared rice with a flavorful fish stew, a meal that Max and I relished. As friends and family dropped by to extend their warm greetings, we socialized briefly before excusing ourselves to retire for the night. Mindful of our impending journey to my parents' village in Bali the following day, we sought to rest and recharge for the road ahead.

Police

"We cannot be separated in interest or divided in purpose."
—African saying

The next morning after breakfast, we rented a car and drove eight hours from my cousin's house in Mutengene to Bali. The journey felt lengthy due to rough roads and countless police checkpoints. Anyone who has traveled within Cameroon will attest to the nuisance of "security checkpoints" on the roads. Sometimes, these checkpoints are less than 10 meters apart. They are variously staffed by police, the "gendarmerie" (French police), a remnant of the French colonial presence and, in my opinion, a French military force on standby, and civilians representing the Department of Transportation, who are charged with enforcing road safety measures. From my observations, it appeared all these representatives were merely there to collect money from bus passengers and drivers. It's widely acknowledged that regardless of one's infractions, whether lacking necessary travel documents, forgetting one's national identity card, neglecting to carry a first aid kit, or exceeding passenger capacity, having money ready to grease palms at various checkpoints ensures smooth passage.

We traveled in a private rental car, and our driver seemed familiar with how to handle the police. At some checkpoints, he would joke and laugh with them; at others, they insisted on bribes. Though bothered by this practice, I remained quiet. During the long drive, my thoughts dwelled on this system of bribing law enforcement, particularly because my father had been a police officer who rose to the rank of Principal Police Commissioner. I wondered whether he had witnessed or been aware of such practices during his tenure. Rumors suggested he retired early because he opposed the emerging culture of bribery within the police corps. He has never confirmed or denied these rumors, as doing so would put him at odds with the government and his former colleagues still in active duty.

As our journey to Bali continued, I couldn't help but notice how "rough" inadequately described the roads and countryside. The streets were lined with incomplete buildings, some abandoned, others under construction. Aging school buildings stood alongside them, while street vendors approaching our car windows at every stop wore expressions of hardship.

As I attempted to process my observations and emotions, I found myself grappling with a mix of excitement and dismay. While the prospect of returning home initially filled me with joy, it gradually gave way to despondency. I realized that my perception of Cameroon was tainted by childhood memories of a vastly different country.

The streets were dustier than I remembered, poverty and hardship more palpable, and the divide between the government and its people wider than I had ever imagined. The police officers we encountered exuded an aura of superiority, bordering on the "godlike." Their demeanor suggested they held the power to dictate our very breaths. They detained numerous drivers for minor or nonexistent infractions, leaving them powerless to protest. Those who dared voice grievances faced prolonged detention.

At one checkpoint, a police officer halted us with a loud whistle, reminiscent of a soccer referee. He sauntered to the car with a lackadaisical air, as if he owned both the vehicle and its occupants. Upon reaching my window, he tapped it and gestured for me to roll it down, which I did promptly. Clad in a faded green khaki uniform with a tilted black beret cap, he scanned the car's interior, scrutinizing us as if playing a silent game of "eeny, meeny, miny, moe" to determine our fates. Selecting me, he demanded my "ID card." I handed him my Cameroon passport, prompting a slightly irritated response as he insisted on seeing an identification card. Calmly, I reminded him that "ID" stood for "Identification," which only seemed to aggravate him further. He proceeded to demand ID cards from all passengers, and while the driver and my cousin presented their Cameroon national ID cards, his focus remained fixed on me.

Snatching their cards from their hands, he held them aloft, casting a stern gaze in my direction as if to impart a lesson on the definition of identification. Turning to my Caucasian friend Max, he requested his ID. Max promptly produced his American passport, receiving a cursory glance before it was returned without comment. After returning the other ID cards, the officer demanded to see my green card, the residence permit that allowed me to legally reside in the

United States at the time. Obliging without hesitation, I handed it over, only to be met with a sharp command to step out of the car, his voice dripping with anger.

He questioned me in French, asking if I thought he was foolish. After a brief pause, I replied calmly that I wasn't entirely sure yet, but I would make that determination once I understood why he wanted me to step out of the car. His expression hardened as he retorted, "I asked for your green card, and you showed me this card?" I fought back the urge to laugh; the irony was almost too much to bear. While the card I had handed him was indeed my green card, it wasn't green in color. The police officer had apparently assumed it should be green or at least labeled "Green Card." Suppressing my amusement, I complied and exited the vehicle, trailing behind him with measured steps. With an air of authority, he led me toward his colleagues gathered around a red Toyota Corolla. Addressing them in French with a smirk, he declared, "We've got a teacher here. Mr. Know-it-all." Their indifferent gazes turned toward me as he handed my documents to one of them, presumably his superior. The senior officer examined my documents, his demeanor composed yet authoritative and inquired about the situation in a firm but calm tone.

As the junior officer recounted the green card incident, I watched his supervisor and the other officers erupt into laughter. Puzzled by their reaction, the junior officer glanced back at me before shifting his focus to the group. He adjusted his hat, questioning what was amusing. Amidst the laughter, the senior officer explained that despite its color, the card I had provided was indeed a green card. The junior officer argued that it lacked the words "Green Card" printed on it, prompting even more laughter. Suppressing a smile, I accepted my returned documents as the senior officer advised me to be courteous to his colleague. I thanked him and began walking back to the car. Before I could depart, the junior officer quipped, "Hey, teacher, make sure you have the right documents next time. You're lucky my boss is in a good mood today." I offered a smile and waved before returning to the car, relieved to leave that checkpoint behind.

As we pressed forward, the stark contrast between my homeland now and the one I had left nine years ago left me utterly perplexed. In my father's era, police officers were regarded as the epitome of intelligence, yet today, I found myself facing an officer who seemed scarcely aware of the travel documents necessary for domestic travel. Perhaps he had secured his position through less-than-savory means, potentially buying his way into the police academy if he had attended at all. Such tales were not uncommon; rumors abounded of individuals resorting to bribery to secure coveted government positions, from law enforcement and customs to education and even the esteemed school of magistracy.

CHAPTER 19

Bali Nyonga

"If you climb up a tree, you must climb down the same tree."
—*African Proverb*

In Chinua Achebe's *Things Fall Apart*, first published in 1958, the story is set in precolonial Nigeria and centers on Okonkwo, a respected leader and warrior in the Igbo community of Umuofia. Achebe's narrative explores the complex social, cultural, and political dynamics of the Igbo people before and during the early days of European colonization. Okonkwo is introduced as a man who has achieved great success through hard work and personal prowess. The customs, traditions, and religious beliefs of Igbo society provide a rich backdrop for the story.

Despite his success, Okonkwo's life is marked by internal and external conflicts. He struggles with his fear of being perceived as weak, like his father, a fear that drives many of his actions. His strict adherence to traditional values often puts him at odds with changing times and the people around him, including his family. After an unfortunate event, Okonkwo is exiled from Umuofia to his mother's village for seven years. During his exile, he works hard, becoming successful and wealthy, yet he longs to return to his father's village.

Upon his return, he realizes time has not stood still. He is no longer the influential figure he expected to be. The peaceful existence of Umuofia has been disrupted by European missionaries and colonial administrators. The introduction of Christianity begins to erode the Igbo people's traditional beliefs and social structures. Okonkwo views the missionaries as a direct threat to the Igbo way of life and responds with increasing hostility. His internal conflicts persist until he wages war on the administrators and hangs himself rather than face justice in the White man's court.

Back in Cameroon, Max, my family members, and I pulled up to my ancestral home to find a throng of eager relatives awaiting our arrival, ready to envelop us in warm embraces. The flood of emotions was so overwhelming that the subsequent hours felt like a blur. Family members came and went; some teenagers who had introduced themselves had been mere children when I departed for America nine years earlier, while certain adults appeared older and more weathered than my memory served. Nevertheless, their presence brought immense joy. After refreshing ourselves with cold showers, we joined the extended family for dinner, a heartwarming reunion after all these years. As we sat in my father's living room, surrounded by familiar faces, I couldn't help but feel nostalgia wash over me. Their curiosity about America was palpable, though I found myself reluctant to delve into details just yet. Around 11 p.m., Max and I bid our goodnights and met with an outpouring of hugs before retiring to our rooms.

The following morning or perhaps closer to midday, I was roused by a resounding knock on the door. It was my father, questioning why I was still in bed. I was taken aback; after all, as a seasoned traveler himself, he should have understood the toll of jet lag. Yet his patriarchal demeanor, asserting control over his clan, prevailed. I cracked the door open, puzzled by his inquiry. He expressed surprise at our late rising, reminding me of the missed church service due to my slumber. His insistence jolted me awake, and I explained our jet-lag-induced fatigue and requested a few days to adjust. Unimpressed, he nodded and informed us that lunch would soon be served, as if he had spent the morning toiling in the kitchen.

I returned to bed, but sleep eluded me. Instead, I lay there, staring at the ceiling, my father's remark about missing church service weighing heavily on my mind.

Growing up, I was raised as a Christian and baptized as an infant in the Catholic Church, a practice that now evokes conflicting emotions. I despise the notion of child baptism, feeling as though I was coerced into a lifelong commitment to an organization I've grown to have little feelings for. I feel trapped by societal expectations; even when I fail to attend Mass, my family never fails to notice and question my absence. Once, my mother reprimanded me sternly for missing service, to which I jokingly responded that I was part of the "secret service"—a quip met with her disapproving silence.

Yet I can't help but admire the shrewdness of the Catholic Church's strategy. By baptizing children at a young age, they effectively secure a future clientele, much like McDonald's enticing children with their addictive fries, ensuring lifelong customers through taste and parental influence.

Although I occasionally attend church for weddings, funerals, or other special occasions, I find myself more preoccupied with thoughts of those around me than with the sermon itself. I often wonder if the preachers truly believe the words they preach or if it's merely rhetoric to appease the masses.

In 2015, while my mother was visiting me in the United States, I took her to the Milwaukee Basilica. After circling for five minutes, we found a parking spot. Stepping out of the car, she adjusted her white Sunday hat, carefully selected for the occasion. She stole a quick glance at her reflection in the tinted car window, nodding in satisfaction. Together, we walked with quiet anticipation toward the imposing double doors of the basilica.

I tried the door, but it seemed locked. My mother met my puzzled look with a determined gaze. Summoning my strength, I tried again, and to our relief, the heavy doors swung open. As we entered, a sense of reverence washed over us, enough to sway even the staunchest skeptic. Our eyes were drawn to the towering ceilings adorned with magnificent paintings of ethereal figures draped in silk and flowers. The color palette was rich—white, gold, and light blue—accentuated by massive marble pillars gilded in gold. The floors and walls gleamed with polished marble, casting a heavenly aura.

My mother took a deep breath, her gaze reflecting the awe of someone entering the gates of heaven. I guided her to a pew toward the back, where a few open spaces remained. At the edge sat a couple, their faces stern and unyielding, as if Satan himself had interrupted their service. With a smile and a whispered "excuse us," we gently eased into the pew, met with hesitant acquiescence from the couple. Though the man nearest the exit appeared affronted, he refrained from causing a scene in the presence of God and the crucified Christ. Reluctantly, they leaned back, granting us silent permission to join the congregation. We settled into our places with reverence, though the woman clutched her purse so tightly her knuckles turned white. The huge organ was playing one of the hymns in praise of Mother Mary.

My mother and I continued to admire the vibrant, colorful ceiling in awe. I eventually shifted my gaze from the ceiling to the audience and quickly noticed that we were one of only two Black families in the entire "kingdom." Even the otherwise homogeneous congregation was composed mostly of senior citizens, from what I could see. I did not notice any children, even among the few young couples in attendance. My thoughts then quickly shifted to the economic situation in the United States at the time.

The American housing market was unforgiving to countless people who were losing their homes for various reasons, and I wondered how many homes the church could save if it sold this magnificent building. I was so lost in thought that I did not realize the collection basket was being passed around to gather more money for the upkeep of the marble and other lavish church belongings. My mother nudged me and handed me a sack with a golden handle, which I quickly grabbed and passed on to the couple next to me, as if it were a hot potato. The woman accepted the sack without looking at me, as her husband stuffed an envelope into it. I wondered how much they had contributed and looked around as several small envelopes disappeared into additional sacks being passed around the church. My experiences in churches have continued to push me further away from organized religion, and I have never discussed this with my parents. That is why they keep asking why I do not attend church.

During my time in Cameroon, I embarked on a journey to revisit familiar places from my youth, seeking to reconcile my memories with the present. Much of my time was spent in my village, reconnecting with my parents and immersing myself in the surroundings.

With some disposable income from saving up for the trip, I set out to reconnect with old friends. However, I soon discovered that many of my former classmates and acquaintances had either relocated or traveled abroad. This realization sparked contemplation on the widespread migration of my generation to foreign countries.

Among these individuals were once-promising students who had excelled in our classes. I couldn't help but wonder about the potential paths they might have pursued back home in Cameroon—perhaps as medical professionals, lawyers, social activists, politicians, successful entrepreneurs, or esteemed educators. Yet here they were, living abroad, their talents and potential enriching distant lands rather than their homeland.

Each day brought a mix of emotions as I encountered both new and familiar faces. One afternoon, while seated on my father's veranda, an old neighborhood friend, seemingly frozen in time, paid a visit. Despite our shared history, I found it challenging to engage in conversation with him. After briefly reminiscing and fielding his inquiries about America, it became apparent that we were on different wavelengths. I navigated his questions delicately, trying to bridge the gap between our experiences.

As more neighbors and family joined us, I asked my sister to fetch some beer to ease the day's heat. With each round, our discussions shifted from local gossip to stories of those who had traveled abroad, urban employment, marriages, local and international soccer tournaments, and eventually, political discourse.

Perhaps fueled by the beer or the growing number of participants, I soon found my ideas and perspectives dismissed as "Western" or "foreign," as if they were incompatible with the Cameroonian context. Repeatedly shot down, I gradually withdrew from the conversation, assuming the role of a silent observer. It was disheartening to realize that despite my education and experiences, I was perceived by those around me as merely an outsider.

Feeling marginalized and misunderstood, I sat in silence, pondering my place in a community that once felt like home. Despite my efforts to reconnect, I couldn't shake the feeling of being cast aside as a mere visitor—a sentiment that weighed heavily on my heart. After observing quietly from the sidelines for some time, I decided to interject and steer the conversation in a different direction. In a casual tone, I posed a question: Could those of us from the diaspora ever truly be considered members of this community again? The veranda fell into an awkward silence, stretching on for what felt like an eternity. Eventually, one of the older visitors cleared his throat and spoke.

He began by expressing gratitude for the beer and the enjoyable time we had shared. With a cautious tone, he apologized in advance for his forthcoming remarks, urging me to disregard anything I found disagreeable while still maintaining respect for him. Then, in a measured voice, he explained that acceptance into the community depended on various factors: how long we stayed, our level of involvement in local activities such as church or politics, and our approach to land ownership.

As he outlined these unspoken conditions, it dawned on me that there were implicit requirements for reclaiming my "citizenship" in the place I once called home. Lost in thought, I glanced around and noticed approving nods and knowing smiles from the others, signaling their tacit agreement. Subsequent contributions from the group reinforced these unwritten expectations, though one visitor offered a more lenient perspective, suggesting I didn't necessarily need to wait as long to regain my agency.

The question of "where is home?" echoed loudly in my mind. Despite my longing for this place, the realization that many viewed my return through a lens of conditional acceptance left me feeling conflicted and unsettled. I could see clearly how Okonkwo in Achebe's *Things Fall Apart* felt when he returned to his father's land after seven years in exile.

CHAPTER 20

My Continued Middle

"All great literature is one of two stories: a man goes on a journey or a stranger comes to town."
—*Leo Tolstoy*

It feels as if I am destined to dwell in the middle. America has been incredibly generous to me, offering boundless opportunities—especially with a doctorate degree and over 20 years of professional experience. Our children are thriving in school, growing up in a safe neighborhood where they form friendships with local kids. Now spread across different schools, from high school to elementary, they enjoy sleepovers and playdates with their classmates. Meanwhile, my wife excels in her career at a hospital, steadily advancing in the food and nutrition department.

During the challenges of the COVID-19 pandemic, I worked remotely while the kids attended virtual school. This prompted us to move to a larger home in the neighboring city of Plover to accommodate our evolving needs. Life in

America is undeniably wonderful, and I feel privileged to call myself an American.

Yet, despite these blessings, I struggle with one lingering question: "Where do I truly belong?" Wole Soyinka, the first Black African recipient of the Nobel Prize in Literature (1986) and a member of Nigeria's Yoruba ethnic group, once posed a thought-provoking question: *"Does the mangrove dwelling in the river make it a crocodile?"* Implicit bias and systemic racism remain formidable barriers for Black men, particularly African immigrants seeking full acceptance in American society. No matter their education, professional achievements, wealth, or any other measure of success, true assimilation often feels out of reach. Not even ascending to the highest office in the land offers immunity from discrimination. Just ask Barack Obama, who shattered historical barriers in 2008 by becoming the nation's first non-white president.

Obama's journey to the presidency was a testament to resilience and determination. Born to a Kenyan father and an American mother, he grew up navigating diverse cultural identities and societal expectations. Despite facing skepticism and prejudice, he pursued higher education at prestigious institutions like Harvard Law School, dedicated himself to community organizing, and ultimately entered politics. His historic candidacy resonated deeply with many, including myself, a newly naturalized citizen and father of biracial children.

However, Obama's candidacy was not without its detractors. Both Black and White communities scrutinized his identity and upbringing, casting doubt on his authenticity and eligibility for the presidency. Some questioned his Blackness, while others propagated baseless conspiracy theories about his citizenship and birthplace. Despite these obstacles, Obama's victory symbolized progress and inspired marginalized communities across the country and the world.

Yet, even as the most powerful individual in the nation, Obama confronted the harsh realities of racism and disrespect. His presidency, though historic, did not mark the end of social and racial injustice in America. Despite significant legislative milestones, including desegregation, civil rights laws, and the election of a Black president, discrimination persists at both individual and institutional levels.

As a Black man in America, I have experienced the insidious manifestations of racism, ranging from subtle biases to overt discrimination. Reflecting on my early days in a small town like Stevens Point, I now recognize the many ways in which prejudice permeated everyday interactions. Whether being conspicuously avoided in a classroom or subjected to unwarranted surveillance in a store, these microaggressions underscore the persistent challenges faced by Black individuals in America.

The consequences of individual biases and institutionalized racism extend far beyond mere inconvenience, often resulting in tragic outcomes, including the loss of life. Despite strides toward equality, the fight against social and racial injustice continues, reminding us that the struggle for true equality is far from over.

In 2014, a distressing 911 call reported a man brandishing what appeared to be a pistol. Notably, the caller also mentioned that the individual in question might be a juvenile and that the weapon could be a toy. Within just twelve minutes of the call, a harrowing incident unfolded in Cleveland,

Ohio, resembling a scene ripped straight from a Hollywood action thriller.

A police cruiser had barely come to a halt when an officer in the passenger seat forcefully kicked open the door, leaping out with his firearm drawn. In the blink of an eye, two shots rang out, and the victim crumpled to the ground, later succumbing to his injuries at the hospital. That victim was Tamir Rice, a 12-year-old African American boy. The officer who fired the fatal shots, 26-year-old Timothy Loehmann, was never criminally charged, a decision that left many grappling with a profound sense of injustice.

The anguish of this case lingers with me, resonating deeply and shaping my perception of law enforcement as an institution. My perspective is colored not only by my own experiences but also by the legacy of my father, who devoted nearly three decades to law enforcement in our native Cameroon.

As a Black man raising biracial children in a predominantly White community in central Wisconsin, navigating the complexities of identity, culture, and belonging is a daily endeavor. My wife, Amy, a White native of Medford, Wisconsin, and I find ourselves constantly shaping our children's identities, guiding them through the nuanced intersections of race, ethnicity, and heritage both within our home and in the broader American society.

We strive to instill in our children a deep sense of self-worth and pride in their diverse heritage. From an early age, they are immersed in both African and American cultures, learning about my African traditions, languages, and customs while also embracing their mother's small-town Midwestern upbringing.

One of our ongoing challenges is helping them navigate the complexities of racial identity in America. Growing up biracial means grappling with questions of belonging and acceptance, as well as confronting stereotypes and prejudices from both within and outside their communities. We work hard to create a safe and nurturing environment where they can embrace their dual heritage without feeling pressured to choose one over the other.

Because their mixed-race identity makes them stand out, we take a proactive approach in addressing instances of discrimination or ignorance, teaching them to be proud of who they are while also advocating for respect and understanding from others. We encourage them to explore and celebrate their unique blend of cultures, whether through family dinners that fuse African and Midwestern cuisine or holidays that honor traditions from both sides of the family.

Education plays a crucial role in shaping our children's perspectives on race and identity. We prioritize teaching them about America's history of race relations, the struggles of marginalized communities, and the importance of empathy and solidarity in the fight for equality. As they grow older, we remain committed to fostering open, honest discussions about race, so they feel comfortable asking questions, expressing their emotions, and navigating their dual identity with confidence and grace.

At the same time, I walk a delicate balance between preparing my children for the challenges they may face as biracial individuals and ensuring that my own experiences do not overshadow their potential. They were born in America, a country where racism and discrimination can manifest in many ways through skin tone, accent, socioeconomic status, and even zip code. I educate them on how to handle encounters with the police, hoping they will never need to use that knowledge.

Sometimes, challenges arise within our extended family. The tragic case of Tamir Rice deeply affected me, leading me to establish a strict rule: no toy guns in our home. However, my children's White grandmother had a different perspective. She allowed them to play with toy guns at her house, but would always preface it in my presence with, "Your father doesn't like guns." Whether she truly didn't grasp the privileges and risks at play or simply found this explanation more convenient, I can't say. But if living in America has taught me anything, it is the profound difference between rights and privilege.

As a Black man, I often question whether I have the same privilege as others to call the police for help. The case of Breonna Taylor in 2020 is a stark example. She and her boyfriend sought protection from law enforcement, only for Breonna to be fatally shot in her own home by the very officers meant to serve and protect. Simply going for a run, like Ahmaud Arbery in 2020, or walking through a neighborhood, like Trayvon Martin in 2012, could cost me my life at the hands of vigilantes emboldened by "stand your ground" laws.

Most White individuals will never fully grasp the mental and emotional toll it takes on a Black man just to step outside his home. There's a constant fear of being pulled over, of making a wrong turn in a predominantly White neighborhood, or of needing help from law enforcement or residents if my car breaks down. There's the anxiety of being followed in stores, of inadvertently appearing suspicious, or of making white women uncomfortable simply by existing in the same space.

Even after living in my community for over 20 years, I still hesitate to venture out alone. I often ask my children to accompany me just to feel safer on a walk or bike ride. It's a cruel irony that in America, I rely on my children's presence not just for comfort, but to appear less threatening to White America, as though their innocence is a shield for my survival. Sometimes, it honestly feels like I can't breathe. There are moments when it feels as if the very air around me is constricting, pressing in with the weight of oppression and injustice.

In the ongoing struggle against systemic racism and police brutality, the Black community employs various avenues to voice our grievances and demand change. Yet, no matter the method, each is met with resistance and condemnation.

Colin Kaepernick, a former NFL quarterback, rose to prominence not only for his athletic talent but also for his courageous stand against racial inequality in the United States. His decision to kneel during the national anthem became a powerful symbol of protest, sparking both admiration and controversy nationwide.

Kaepernick's protest began in 2016 when he first chose to sit during the national anthem to protest police brutality and racial injustice. His actions quickly drew national attention, igniting a fierce debate about the role of athletes in speaking out against social issues. In an interview, he explained, *"I am not going to stand up to show pride in a flag for a country that oppresses Black people and people of color."*

As the protest gained traction, it took on even greater significance during the 2016 presidential election. Supporters praised Kaepernick's courage, while detractors accused him of disrespecting the flag and the military. President Trump seized on the controversy, condemning Kaepernick's actions and calling for NFL owners to fire players who knelt during the anthem.

Despite relentless backlash, Kaepernick remained steadfast in his mission to highlight racial inequality. He pledged to donate $1 million to organizations working in oppressed communities and launched the *Know Your Rights Camp*, an initiative dedicated to educating and empowering youth of color about their rights.

His impact extended far beyond the football field, inspiring athletes across multiple sports to use their platforms for social change. His influence resonated throughout popular culture, sparking conversations about racial justice among celebrities, activists, and ordinary citizens alike.

Years after his initial protest, Kaepernick's legacy continues to evolve. While he has not played in the NFL since the 2016 season, his advocacy remains a defining aspect of his identity. He has become a symbol of resistance and resilience, a reminder of the ongoing struggle for equality in America. As the nation grapples with issues of race and justice, Kaepernick stands as proof that change requires courage, conviction, and a willingness to confront uncomfortable truths.

Critics often dismiss our cries for justice by pointing out that police violence also affects White individuals. But the acceptance of such brutality in one community does not justify or diminish the pain and fear experienced by another. Living as a Black person in America often feels like being a gazelle navigating a treacherous jungle—constantly dodging threats just to make it through another day. Some days, the weight of oppression is suffocating, leaving us gasping for air, desperate to breathe.

Remember:

In 2019, Derrick Scott said, **"I can't breathe!"**

In 2019, Javier Amber II said, **"I can't breathe!"**

In 2019, Christopher Lowe said, **"I can't breathe!"**

In 2019, John Neville said, **"I can't breathe!"**

In 2020, Manuel Ellis said, **'I can't breathe!"**

In 2020, George Floyd said, **"I can't breathe!"**

In 2014, Eric Gardner said, **"I can't breathe!"** 8 times!!!

In 2019, Byron William said, **"I can't breathe!"** 24 times!!!

As I've grown older and gained more experience in America, I've found that individual instances of discrimination weigh less heavily on my mind than the systemic injustices deeply embedded within our institutions. Kimberlé Crenshaw and others coined the term *Critical Race Theory* (CRT) to describe a framework for understanding and addressing racial inequality and injustice across various fields, including law, education, healthcare, and business. Its practical applications involve critically examining existing systems and policies to promote equity and justice for marginalized racial and ethnic groups. Sadly, CRT has become a buzzword for politicians seeking to uphold the status quo and continue the subjugation of minority communities.

Since my initial trip to Cameroon with Max in 2010, I've made numerous trips there. In honor of my sister, Ma Kah Rosemary, I founded the Makah Foundation, with a mission to construct 40 pump wells to provide clean drinking water. Each well symbolizes a year of her life on this earth. Over time, the Makah Foundation has evolved into an organization dedicated to aiding women and children. We've established an orphanage and resource center to support those displaced by Cameroon's ongoing civil conflict.

Returning to America is always hard on my psyche. As I waited at the airport in Cameroon for my departure to the United States in 2013, I found myself reflecting on my life. Despite the unwritten "conditions" required to reclaim my Cameroonian "citizenship," I realized that finding a sense of belonging is much easier in my native village of Bali, Cameroon, than in America or in my small city of Stevens Point and Plover, Wisconsin.

In Bali, my surname carries weight, and I effortlessly navigate social interactions, contributing to society through both my academic expertise and life experiences, even if full acceptance might take some time. As I sat at the airport in Douala, pondering my return to America, I struggled to justify going back to a place where I'm constantly questioned about my origins.

In America, I am always on alert about where to go, hoping to avoid any encounters with the police. The dichotomy between the deep roots of belonging in Bali, Cameroon, and the perpetual sense of otherness in America weighed heavily on my mind.

As I sat in the airport waiting room, a vivid recollection of a pivotal day, one that holds immense significance for any immigrant embarking on the journey to American citizenship, flooded my mind. It was 2010, and my wife, Amy, my mother, who lived with us at the time, and our two children had embarked on a journey to Minneapolis the previous day, where my cousin Judith and her family graciously hosted us in their modest yet tastefully furnished apartment.

Throughout that preceding night, I pored over the question book issued by the immigration office, diligently preparing for the impending interview that would determine my eligibility for citizenship. With utmost dedication, I absorbed the book's 100 questions, which covered every aspect of American history. Additionally, I diligently listened to the immigration office's accompanying tape, ensuring I was thoroughly prepared for the challenges ahead. As dawn broke, we dressed in our finest attire and made our way to the interview venue. With grace and ease, I navigated the interview questions and passed without a hitch. Following the interview, we were directed to a hall bustling with excitement, filled with several other families eagerly anticipating their impending naturalization as US citizens.

Seated among rows of soon-to-be citizens from diverse corners of the globe, I marveled at the kaleidoscope of languages echoing through the room. Suddenly, a hush fell over the crowd as a distinguished gentleman, later revealed to be a judge, made his entrance. Taking center stage, he extended warm greetings on behalf of President George Bush and expressed his enthusiasm for the occasion. With a sense of camaraderie, he played a heartfelt video message from the president, congratulating us on this significant milestone and imparting words of wisdom regarding our newfound responsibilities as American citizens. The room erupted into applause as the video concluded, and with hearts brimming with pride and anticipation, it was time for us to take the oath of citizenship.

We were asked to stand and repeat after the judge:

"I hereby declare, on oath, that I absolutely and entirely renounce and abjure all allegiance and fidelity to any foreign

prince, potentate, state, or sovereignty, of whom or which I have heretofore been a subject or citizen; that I will support and defend the Constitution and laws of the United States of America against all enemies, foreign and domestic; that I will bear true faith and allegiance to the same; that I will bear arms on behalf of the United States when required by the law; that I will perform noncombatant service in the Armed Forces of the United States when required by the law; that I will perform work of national importance under civilian direction when required by the law; and that I take this obligation freely, without any mental reservation or purpose of evasion; so help me God."

As those words left my lips, especially when I had to renounce my Cameroon citizenship, a sense of betrayal and emptiness washed over me. It echoed the poignant scene from the 1977 TV show *Roots*, where the young black slave, Kunta Kinte, is brutally beaten and coerced into relinquishing his name, accepting his new identity as "Tobi." While I wasn't subjected to physical violence or coercion, the weight of surrendering my allegiance was palpable. It felt like a voluntary, yet inevitable act of resignation, leaving a hollow ache in my heart.

It was no surprise that I was sitting at the airport in Cameroon three years later, contemplating whether to return or not. I slowly concluded that calling Amy back to tell her I wasn't coming would devastate her, but I hoped she would understand and forgive me. My mind was a whirlwind of thoughts in that airport waiting room in Cameroon, each vying for attention as I reminisced about another significant day from 2007.

It was a day etched into memory when Amy and I were strolling through the bustling downtown mall in Stevens

Point, and her voice broke the ordinary with the magical words, "My water broke." In a rush of adrenaline-fueled urgency, we made a beeline for the hospital, a mere 35-minute drive away in a neighboring city where Amy worked. The labor and delivery process itself could fill the pages of another book entirely, a tale of anticipation and uncertainty that defies any amount of preparation from videos or clinic visits. In the delivery room, a symphony of activity unfolded as nurses and aides bustled about, their movements choreographed with precision. Occasional visits from the doctor marked the progress, while Amy's determination to bring our child into the world was insurmountable with each push. As I stood by her side, my role fluctuated between offering support and capturing the moment with the camera clenched tightly in my hand. Then, without any warning, things started moving fast, and I was asked to make way. The nurses became more urgent yet composed as they went about their duties.

The doctor was called in again, and I knew it was happening. The doctor came, fired a few orders, and got into position. The lighting and seating were all done like a well-choreographed dance between the nurses and the doctor. The doctor encouraged Amy to keep pushing. I took a position strategically around her head, partly to stay out of the way and partly to avoid any blood because I tend to get light-headed at the sight of blood. She continued pushing every so often. She asked for a wet rag, which was promptly provided. One of the nurses entrusted the cold rag duty to me, which I dutifully complied with. I kept dabbing her forehead with one hand and expertly clutched the camera in the other, ready to immortalize the moment. Amy thanked me for the cold rag and, in less than two minutes, scolded me about "putting a cold rag" on her head. The nurses, without missing a beat, grabbed the rag, and it disappeared.

I had been encouraged to also assist with the "push and blow." This is when, between pushes, you encourage the mother to breathe rhythmically through her mouth. So, I kept up with the breathing exercise. After one of the major pushes, I encouraged her to do the blowing exercise again, and apparently, this seemed to be the worst thing to say. She screamed at me and reminded me it was my fault that she was in this pain in the first place.

Then the doctor got even more serious, and I saw the baby's head. The good doctor reached in and gently performed a pull-and-spin maneuver. The entire face was out as a nurse scrambled with a suction apparatus to clear mucus from the nose and mouth to allow the baby to breathe. The doctor continued the spin-and-pull dance again, this time to clear the shoulder blades. Once that was achieved, the rest of the baby seemed to glide out without much effort, at least not on my part. A nurse attached a couple of clamps to both sides of the umbilical cord. Then I was invited to cut the cord, separating mother and child. As I completed the task, I was so overwhelmed with joy and excitement that the adrenaline made my body shake. I was shaking so badly that the doctor asked me to sit down. I was helped to a nearby seat by one of the nurses.

The doctor grabbed the baby in one hand as he expertly cleaned the mouth and nose again, then flipped the baby on its back and gave it a tap. The baby squeaked and shivered. A nurse brought over a warm towel, wrapped the baby, and handed him to Amy. She cried as she clutched the baby in her arms. It was a beautiful sight. I walked over and joined my new family.

We named our son, Sivan, which means the ninth month of the ecclesiastical year on the Hebrew calendar, and Sigala, which in my language means "I am responsible for my decisions." In my ethnic group, most middle names are intended for the parents rather than the child. We had agreed that if we had a boy, his name would have my initials, SS, and, if it were a girl, AL for Amy Lynn.

Sivan was a very happy and handsome child. I spent a lot of time with him and connected with him at different levels. When he was about four years old, an incident happened that almost destroyed my life and, most importantly, my relationship with my son.

It was a winter Monday morning. By this time, we had a second child, Sander, who was about two years old. I had a very important meeting at work at 8 a.m. I woke up around 6:45 a.m. and looked over my PowerPoint presentation. I shaved, took a warm shower, and got dressed. I usually did not eat breakfast, so I just sat in the living room and let the kids sleep as long as I could without being late. Then, at about 7:15 a.m., I woke the kids up and got them ready for daycare. Sivan, excited to go to daycare, decided without warning that he wasn't going. He sat on the steps and would not move. I stepped outside and started the car to warm it up. When I came back to pick up the kids, Sivan continued his sit-down strike. I bundled his brother in his car seat and took him to the car. I walked back in the house, and he was still in the same position. I pleaded with him and threatened endless timeouts, but he would not move.

I threatened to leave him alone in the house. I left the house again, went and sat with Sander in the car for about five minutes. I could see the clock ticking away, and I knew I was going to be late for my meeting. I walked back to the house, seized him, and gave him a two-finger slap on his right cheek. He took off running to the car. I followed him, and we rode the short ride to the daycare building. I dropped them off and had this terrible feeling in my stomach. I went to work and did my best with the presentation. As soon as I was done with the presentation, I told my supervisor that I was not feeling well and would like to take the rest of the day off. He obliged, and I headed home.

I sat on the couch and played the scene over and over till the doorbell rang. My heart skipped. I came to the door, and there was a lady and a police officer I knew from the community. The lady introduced herself as a caseworker from child protective services. She asked me if I was Sivan Dinga's father. The police officer greeted me by name and asked if they could come inside. I let them in, and we sat down in the living room. The lady scanned the room as she spoke. She explained that Sivan's teacher noticed the fingerprints on his cheek and called her office, and with the head marks, they are required to respond with a police officer.

My heart continued to race. She asked me what had happened. I kept calm and spoke as slowly as I could, my mouth dry. I narrated what had happened in the morning. When I finished speaking, the police officer spoke first. He cleared his throat and said my story was the same as my son had explained to them. The social worker added that Sivan said he did it just to upset me and that he thought it was fun. I calmly asked if I was going to jail and if my kids would be taken away. They both said "no" simultaneously. The social worker explained that I had no prior complaints against me, that my story was the same as Sivan's, and that my neighbor had vouched for my character. She concluded that I would only have to attend anger management class on a date and at a place of my choosing. I agreed to meet at my house a few weeks later.

It was a difficult time for my relationship with Sivan, as I could not help but realize that a simple reaction like that could have easily landed me on the treadmill of the US criminal justice system. A system that has more people incarcerated than the population of Belize, Tonga, Saint Lucia, and Guam combined.

I was deep in my thoughts as I sat at the airport in Cameroon, replaying these incidents and wondering whether to return. My phone vibrated in my chest pocket and brought me to consciousness. I had a photo of Amy holding Sivan as a screensaver when she called from her cell phone. I stared at the phone for what seemed like ages before answering.

"Hello," I said in a very hoarse voice and struggled to clear my throat.

"Daddy," Sivan said on the other end. "When are you coming home?"

EPILOGUE

Real Belonging

"A person is a person through other persons."
—*African, Zulu Saying*

The epilogue of this book examines complex immigrant experiences in the United States, drawing on scholarly research on themes such as social integration, cultural adaptation, identity development, and psychological well-being. Through a synthesis of academic literature and personal anecdotes, this epilogue aims to illuminate the diverse challenges and triumphs immigrants face as they navigate a new cultural landscape. By delving into these multifaceted themes, we can gain a deeper appreciation for the complexities of immigrant experiences and the factors that shape their sense of belonging in their adopted homeland.

Social integration studies focus on immigrants' social connections and interactions within their host communities. Research indicates that social integration plays a crucial role in fostering a sense of belonging among immigrants. This includes participation in community activities, forming friendships with locals, and joining social networks. I found it relatively easy to integrate into American society, especially in my small city of Stevens Point. Several factors contributed to this, including my extroverted personality, which enabled me to connect effortlessly with others.

Additionally, the "Host Family" program at the University of Wisconsin-Stevens Point played a significant role in facilitating my social integration. The Okray family, my designated host family, provided me with a sense of belonging and inclusion. They welcomed me into their home as often as my schedule allowed, accompanied me to various community events, and introduced me to their social circles, treating me as a cherished member of their family.

Similarly, I formed a close bond with John and Patty Noel, who embraced me as one of their children, inviting me to their gatherings and offering invaluable guidance and support throughout my journey in America. I met John at a university function, where I saw him from across the room listening to someone. I observed how intensely he was listening to this person without interrupting. I had never seen such intense listening before, so sometime during the night I found my way to him and introduced myself. He said his name was John Noel, and then I asked him to teach me how to listen. This was the start of a long-term friendship between the Noels and me. John's mentorship and connections in the community expanded my social network and exposed me to new opportunities. I am immensely grateful to the Noel family for their generosity and unwavering support, which have played a pivotal role in my integration and growth in Stevens Point.

For work, I interviewed with the Boys & Girls Club, which specializes in youth programming. I barely knew what they did, but the director at the time who conducted the interview saw something in me and gave me a chance. He became my boss, my mentor and my friend. Kevin and I have stayed close friends, and our wives like to talk to each other. My friendship with Kevin really helped me understand the "real world," as they say. Our age difference allowed Kevin to be another big brother in my life in America.

Lastly, my in-laws, Tom and Lorna, have been a great source of support to my family and me. They supported us immensely with childcare whenever I traveled to Cameroon in the early years of our two boys' lives. They also provided us with meat, corn, eggs, milk, and other items. My kids love them greatly. I will forever be indebted to Tom and Lorna for their love and support.

Cultural Adaptation: Immigrants often navigate multiple cultural identities as they adapt to life in the United States. Research highlights the importance of acculturation strategies in shaping their sense of belonging. While some individuals adopt aspects of the dominant culture, others maintain strong ties to their heritage. The process of bicultural adaptation, where individuals integrate elements of both cultures into their identity, is associated with a greater sense of belonging and well-being.

While I long for the day I can return to Cameroon and find my place, my brother, Ni Ben, is content with his life in America and has firmly established himself in Springfield, Illinois. His deep sense of belonging in his adopted home has always puzzled me. I often wonder why he feels so rooted while I continue to wrestle with my own sense of place.

Despite my active involvement in various community organizations, hoping to cultivate a stronger connection, I still find myself caught between two worlds, never fully belonging to either, no matter how much time passes.

Unfortunately, the nearest Cameroonian community for me is a two-hour drive to Milwaukee or a four-hour journey to Minnesota. Despite the distance, I have made a concerted effort to participate in cultural groups in Minnesota, which allows me to stay connected to my Cameroonian roots every month. This not only helps me preserve my cultural heritage but also provides my children with opportunities to engage with their ancestry.

During these gatherings, I immerse myself in traditional regalia, indulge in delicious African cuisine, play drums, and dance to music that resonates with my heritage. These experiences help fill the emotional void that inevitably resurfaces during my long rides back to Wisconsin.

As an immigrant, I sometimes face discrimination and social exclusion, which can undermine my sense of belonging. Numerous studies show that prejudice, stereotyping, and marginalization affect an individual's psychological adjustment and integration. Discrimination based on race, ethnicity, language, or immigration status creates barriers to belonging and limits opportunities for social participation.

Despite the significant cost and time required to become a U.S. citizen, I was fortunate to navigate the process relatively smoothly. Being a U.S. citizen has always been an honor I deeply cherish. I vividly remember the pride I felt the first time I cast a vote, a duty I took very seriously. On that memorable day in 2008, I took the day off work, dressed in a suit, and had my two young sons wear suits and ties as well. After voting, we celebrated by going out to eat, honoring the privilege of voting and paying tribute to those who paved the way for me, as a Black man in America, to exercise this fundamental right.

Many immigrants maintain connections with their home countries through transnational practices such as sending remittances, communicating with family members, and participating in cultural traditions. Research suggests that these ties can both strengthen and complicate an immigrant's sense of belonging. While they provide emotional support and a sense of connection, they may also lead to feelings of dislocation or cultural hybridity.

My work with the Makah Foundation, which I founded in honor of my sister, Ma Kah Rosemary, keeps me deeply connected to Cameroon. I regularly communicate with the workers at the orphanage I established, raising and wiring funds for its upkeep. While these efforts give me a sense of purpose, they also leave me feeling inadequate, as I constantly wonder whether I am doing enough for the children at the orphanage and others in Cameroon. Additionally, the time I spend fundraising and gathering supplies often makes me feel guilty for not being fully present in the United States.

Access to supportive social networks, community organizations, and institutional resources plays a crucial role in fostering a sense of belonging among immigrants. Research highlights how schools, workplaces, religious institutions, and community-based organizations provide spaces for immigrants to connect, build social capital, and access essential services. Programs that promote cultural competency, language acquisition, and immigrant rights advocacy significantly contribute to their integration and sense of belonging.

I have benefited from several community organizations and social networks, which have helped me form meaningful friendships with people who continue to mentor and advocate for me in various aspects of life.

Today, I find myself standing at the intersection of two worlds, neither of which I can fully claim as my own. The United States, with its promise of opportunity and freedom, has given me a new lens through which to see the world, yet it has also been a source of profound isolation. My homeland of Cameroon, rich with memories and traditions, now feels like a distant echo—a place where I no longer fit seamlessly.

W.E.B. Du Bois introduced the concept of *twoness* in *The Souls of Black Folk*, describing the internal struggle of African Americans who navigate both their Black identity and their American nationality. He describes the feeling of being caught between two worlds, "two souls, two thoughts, two unreconciled strivings" as one seeks to find a unified sense of self. As an immigrant in the United States, I constantly feel the idea of *twoness*, as I try to balance my cultural heritage with the pressure to assimilate into American society despite my 20-plus years living in the United States. I feel torn between maintaining the traditions, language, and values of my homeland while also striving to fit into my adopted cultural landscape. This internal conflict sometimes leads to a sense of displacement, as I sometimes feel neither fully accepted in my adopted country nor completely connected to my origins. Perhaps, for me, overcoming *twoness* will continue to involve creating a blended identity that embraces both cultures, finding strength in duality rather than division.

In this liminal space, I have come to understand that belonging is not about conforming to a single identity or place;

it is about embracing the mosaic of experiences that shape who we are. I continue to weave together the threads of my past and present, creating a tapestry that is uniquely mine. The struggle, the feeling of in-betweenness, is not a weakness but a testament to my resilience and adaptability.

I now realize that home is not a fixed location but a state of being. It is found in the connections I make, the stories I share, and the love I give and receive. I have accepted that I do not have to choose one home over the other; I can belong to both worlds while forging a path that is authentically mine. In the end, my journey is not about fitting into a pre-existing mold but about creating a space where I can be true to myself.

Acknowledgments

This project has been over two years in the making, and it has finally crossed the finish line thanks to several instrumental people.

Dr. Trisha Lamers: My friend and mentor, you were the first person to read this manuscript. You helped me navigate the crucial question of what I truly wanted to address in these pages and pushed me to explore the profound complexities of belonging. Thank you for introducing me to the concept of "matterness." I am forever grateful for your time, your mentorship, and your friendship.

Mr. Martin Jumbam: My editor, who provided a thorough and thoughtful review. Your insights were vital in keeping the narrative focused and cohesive. Thank you for your kind encouragement throughout the editorial process and for suggesting the inclusion of photographs, which have truly brought the print edition to life.

As a first-time author, I needed all the guidance I could get. I received immense support from the team at Spears Books, particularly from the executive publisher, Dr. Jude Fokwang. Thank you for creating this vital avenue for debut authors to navigate the intricacies of the publishing world.

Ba Fonachu Munawoe Fokum: Beyond being my favorite cousin, you led the way in researching our complex family history. Your dedication allowed me to succinctly share my roots and articulate the powerful pull I feel toward Bali Nyonga and Cameroon at large.

Amy Dinga: Finally, I want to express my deepest gratitude to my dear wife Amy for your unwavering support throughout the laborious process of researching, writing, and publishing this book. I hope you see this work as a meaningful reflection of the life we have built together. Thank you for always standing by me through my many adventures.

Without the contributions of these individuals, *Living in the Middle: A Life between Belonging and Becoming* would not have been possible.

About the author

Sam Dinga, Ed.D., began his academic journey studying Law and Political Science at the University of Dschang before moving to the U.S. in 2002. He went on to earn a bachelor's degree in Sociology and a master's in Human & Community Resources from the University of Wisconsin–Stevens Point and later completed his doctorate in Higher Education Leadership at Edgewood University.

Driven by a profound commitment to service, Sam founded the Makah Foundation in memory of his late sister, Makah Rosemary Dinga. Today, he resides with his wife, Amy, and their five children. When he isn't working, Sam is an avid reader and political observer who enjoys unwinding with action movies and firing up the grill for friends and family.

About the Publisher

Spears Books is an independent publisher dedicated to providing innovative publication strategies with emphasis on Africana stories and perspectives. As a platform for alternative voices, we prioritize the accessibility and affordability of our titles to ensure that relevant and often marginal voices are represented in the global marketplace of ideas. Our titles – poetry, fiction, narrative nonfiction, memoirs, reference, travel writing, African languages, and young people's literature – aim to bring African worldviews closer to diverse readers. Our titles are distributed in paperback and electronic formats globally by African Books Collective.

Connect with Us: Go to www.spearsbooks.org to learn about exclusive previews and read excerpts of new books, find detailed information on our titles, authors, subject area books, and special discounts.

Subscribe to our Free Newsletter: Be amongst the first to hear about our newest publications, special discount offers, news about bestsellers, author interviews, coupons and more! Subscribe to our newsletter by visiting www.spearsbooks.org

Quantity Discounts: Spears Books are available at quantity discounts for orders of ten or more copies. Contact Spears Books at orders@spearsmedia.com.

Host a Reading Group: Learn more about how to host a reading group on our website at www.spearsbooks.org

www.ingramcontent.com/pod-product-compliance
Lightning Source LLC
Chambersburg PA
CBHW022055050726
47591CB00002B/546